BEN K. GREEN

a bibliography

Ben K. Green
photograph courtesy of *The Color of Horses*

BEN K. GREEN

A descriptive bibliography of writings by and about him

Compiled by Robert A. Wilson

with a foreword by Jenkins Garrett

Northland Press / Flagstaff

FIRST EDITION

ISBN 0-87358-160-1
Library of Congress Catalog Card Number 76-52541
Composed and Printed in the United States of America

To my dear Jane, for the second time

and

to the memory of the great story tellers from Aesop to Homer to the present, with whom Doc Green is no doubt happily swapping yarns

Contents

Illustrations

Foreword

THERE DOES NOT come to mind any bibliography I have encountered which is more satisfying than this work, written and compiled by my friend, Bob Wilson.

Most bibliographies are stark listings of an author's works, with form and content dictated by academic custom and the technical cataloging of the Library of Congress. This book is much more. There are judicious selections of passages from Green's own writings, and excerpts from the many book reviews, and articles (even obituaries) about Green which appeared in newspapers and magazines over the country. Wilson comments on his own dealings with the old horse trader and gives hints to collectors of Green's writings, with some insights into their publishing history. Such things are above and beyond the scope of formal bibliography, but they make for informative and delightful reading.

'Doc' Green was, to borrow a folklorist's term, a "happening." His dress, his listenable voice, his gift of talk, placed him center stage in any gathering. I always thoroughly enjoyed listening to his pungent comments ("I am seldom misunderstood," he noted) on artists who painted horses standing or running in what he deemed impossible postures; on Barbara Walters and their TV confrontation on the "Today Show"; and his unabashed boast that he never took Dale Carnegie's course on "How to Win Friends and Influence People."

I have never been able to visualize Ben Green as a "writer" in the usual literary sense. He *talked* his books, a fact that accounts, I think, for a good part of their attractiveness. He was an expert narrator, and his "talk" has been caught and preserved in print with great fidelity.

Ben explained that in putting together a book he created one chapter at a time. First he would decide on a general subject. As an appropriate incident came to mind which he deemed worthy of a chapter, he would think about it for a few days. When he had it all in his mind, he would lean back in his office chair with his feet on the desk and dictate the entire chapter to his secretary. She would type a draft, and read it back to him aloud, making necessary corrections as they went along. When it finally sounded right to him, the chapter was sent to the publisher, and thereafter no editorial changes were permitted.

Green's intolerance of attempts to "correct" the language of his typescripts is well known to his publishers and their editors, and is amply evidenced in the copies of his correspondence now housed, along with his manuscripts, page proofs and other papers, in the library of the Arlington campus of the University of Texas.

Ben Green spent his youth and manhood in the horse-and-cattle country. It was his world, and he had a deep love for and commitment to it. It will never return, but he has re-created it for us, with a genius for recall of details and an acceptable leavening of imagination, in his stories and books. I confidently submit that Ben would have been glad to associate himself in the compiling of this book about them.

JENKINS GARRETT

Preface

BEN K. ("DOC") GREEN was born on March 5, 1912, in the village of Cumby, Hopkins County, Texas. He died on October 5, 1974, of a heart attack while driving alone through Kansas on his way back to his home in Cumby.

This bibliography of Green's writing was compiled, with numerous interruptions, during the last two years and more. It aims at being as complete and definitive as any author-bibliography can hope to be, when written this close to the end of its subject's writing career.

Certain difficulties presented themselves. Doc Green had claimed to have written articles on plant toxicology and the food-poisoning of livestock, based upon research he conducted in South America, Central America, Africa, and other far-flung places. But no trace of such articles, if they exist at all, has turned up so far. They have, perforce, been omitted.

Again, there has been a constant temptation to inject some of the more colorful incidents in Green's life history, as they have come to my attention from several sources of varying authenticity, including Doc Green himself. I have resisted the temptation to provide any more biographical details than are necessary to supplement the story of his writings. A full scale biography — and an interesting one it would be — must await a biographer with more time, patience, and perseverance than are available to me at present. I am informed that there is at least one biography in the chute, and perhaps one or two more in the round-up stage. Let's hope they make it all the way into the corral.

I have, however, taken the liberty of interpolating from time to time some observations growing out of my own personal dealings with the old horse trader at my book shop or at the various bookish gatherings where we happened to meet. In every case these meetings were memorable to me — one does not forget encounters with an unshaven story-telling genius.

And now a word about this book. In Part I, I have attempted to list and describe every published work written by Ben K. Green, including magazines, broadsides, ephemeral material, and, of course, books, all in the approximate order of their first publication. And because what the critics have said about his writings is sometimes almost as interesting as the writings themselves, I have appended to the description of each major work a selected list of the reviews it received, with quotations from the more colorful or perceptive of them. I do not claim that this listing includes *all* the reviews written about Green's work; there are undoubtedly a number which have not come to my attention. There are enough, however, to indicate the widespread acceptance and popularity his books enjoyed at the hands of both critics and the public; few indeed must be the southwestern authors whose books have achieved from a major New York publisher the accolade of a *fifteenth* printing!

Part II contains a listing of general articles *about* Green and his colorful life-style, apart from his writings, which appeared in various newspapers and magazines during his life, together with excerpts from a number of them.

Part III contains a listing and quotations from the many obituaries written following his death in 1974. In neither case is there a claim of completeness.

An explanation of certain conventional signs, symbols and abbreviations used by bibliographers in describing books may not be out of place here. The *slant mark* / indicates the end of a line of type on the original page. *Small roman* numerals, i, ii, vi, etc. are used to number the preliminary pages, or "prelims," preceding the main body of the text. *Brackets* [ ] around a number mean that the number does not actually appear in the original; for example [iv] appearing in the "collation" or page-by-page counting, would indicate that the fourth preliminary page in the book is not numbered. Brackets around words or phrases are also used to indicate that the enclosed material does not appear in the original, as when the bibliographer wishes to interrupt an author's text with a comment or explanation of his own. "Recto" refers to the right-hand page of an open book; "verso" to the left-hand page. "Octavo," abbreviated 8vo, means a book the size of a standard modern novel; "quarto" (4TO) means a large book, and duodecimo (12MO) a small one.

Part 1

WRITINGS BY BEN K. GREEN AND THEIR REVIEWS IN THE PRESS

¶ 1 *The International Quarter Horse Tally Book*. Magazine, a complete file in nineteen issues, 8½ by 11 inches, various dates as below, 1960–1962, San Angelo and Fort Worth, Texas.

In 1955 Ben Green and a number of quarter horse owners and breeders organized the "International Quarter Horse Jockey Club." Green was the "executive secretary-treasurer," with headquarters in the lobby of the Cactus Hotel in San Angelo, Texas. As a medium for communication among the members, and to provide a registry for quarter horse owners in Canada and Mexico, as well as in the United States, the club sponsored the publication of a monthly magazine entitled *The International Quarter Horse Tally Book,* with Green as editor, publisher, and contributor.

The first issue appeared in February, 1960, and publication as a monthly magazine continued through the issue for April, 1961, when it became a quarterly as noted below. There was one break, however; the issue for September 1960 was skipped, necessitating the publication of an apology which appeared in the next (October) issue.

In November of 1960 Green moved the Jockey Club and the publication office of *The Tally Book* to Fort Worth, and the December 1960 and subsequent issues were published in that city. But competition from well-established quarter horse magazines was keen, subscriptions were slow, and advertising revenue dwindled. By the spring of 1961 Green was forced to publish *The Tally Book* as a quarterly. Accordingly, the final five issues are dated Summer and Fall, 1961, and Winter, Spring, and Fall, 1962.

In dimensions and outward appearance *The Tally Book* resembled the older issues of *Time* magazine, with a brightly colored border around the front cover and a photograph of a horse and its owner featured in a cover story on the inside. It was printed on coated paper, and contained as many as thirty-five pages, although some issues had as few as eight, depending, of course, upon the amount of advertising space Green was able to sell and the length of the articles written by contributors.

Green's own contributions comprised approximately half the contents. They were of three kinds.

First there were technical articles on the anatomy of the horse, written, as Green said, "down to the language level of a twelve year-old," and designed to aid an owner or prospective buyer in choosing the best type of horse for the work it was expected to perform. A collection of these articles from *The Tally Book* was later published separately under the title *Horse Conformation*.

Second, Green contributed accounts of numerous horse shows, races, auctions and rodeos around the country, at many of which he served as a judge or auctioneer.

But his third and best-known contributions were the delightfully told stories of his early experiences as a young horse trader, cowboy and veterinarian, which appeared in *The Tally Book* under the heading "Hoss Trades of Yesteryear, That Took Place at Wagon Yards and Trade Days, by 'Doc' Green." It is ironic that they were used as fillers to pad out what would otherwise have been blank pages in *The Tally Book*. To Ben's surprise, and somewhat to his chagrin — for he was proud of the technical horse knowledge displayed in the Horse Conformation articles — readers found these stories the best part of

The International Quarter Horse Tally Book—No. 8, October, 1960

The Tally Book. "Comments were numerous and favorable as to this part of the magazine, and I heard many times more about it than . . . about my articles on conformation and soundness of a performance horse," he wrote later in *How Come I Wrote a Book,* one of the volumes in *Ben Green Tales.*

Fifteen of these adventures appeared in the nineteen issues of *The Tally Book,* there being none in the first two and last two issues. Nor did the stories have individual titles; all appeared under the general heading mentioned above.

In 1963 Green published all the stories, plus a new one entitled "The School Marm an Ol' Nothin' " in the back section of his privately printed cloth-bound *Horse Conformation* [*and*] *Hoss Trades of Yesteryear*. For book publication Green found it necessary to give each story an appropriate title. This he did, and the title has stayed with the story throughout subsequent publication, notably *Horse Tradin'* by Alfred A. Knopf, New York.

The following is a complete chronological listing of the nineteen issues of *The International Quarter Horse Tally Book*. It includes all contributions which could be identified as having been written by Green himself; contributions by others have been omitted. For convenience I have shortened "Hoss Trades of Yesteryear" to *Hoss Trades,* and *Horse Tradin'* to *H. Tradin'*.

No. 1, February, 1960. (a) "The Old Tally Book" [An Introduction to the new magazine]; (b) "Here's Why About Shoulders."

No. 2, March, 1960. (a) "Gid Reding, The Greatest Horse 'Charmer' of This or Any Other Age"; (b) "All About Hocks"; (c) "An Editorial [On the increasing scarcity of horses]"; (d) "Guest of the Month: The Hackney."

No. 3, April, 1960. (a) *Hoss Trades*. Story, later published in *H. Tradin'* as "The Rock Crusher and the Mule"; (b) "Forelegs."

No. 4, May, 1960. (a) *Hoss Trades*. In *H. Tradin'* as "Homer's

Last Mule"; (b) "A Whirlwind Inspection Trip Through Kansas and Oklahoma"; (c) "Harmon Baker — A Great Racehorse and Successful Sire."

No. 5, June, 1960. (a) *Hoss Trades.* In *H. Tradin'* as "Matched Mares."

No. 6, July, 1960. (a) "Summer Inspection in Montana"; (b) *Hoss Trades.* In *H. Tradin'* as "Mule Colts"; (c) "Let's Give the 'Forward Seat' Full Credit."

No. 7, August, 1960. (a) "You Can Tell a Lot From the Top Line. The story of a horse's 'Top Line' can give you a quick index to his way of treling [*sic*]"; (b) " 'Great Threat' Measures up to His Pedigree"; (c) *Hoss Trades.* In *H. Tradin'* as "A Road Horse for a Brood Mare."

No. 8. October, 1960 [the September issue was skipped by Green]. (a) "Let's Talk About S-T-R-I-D-E; Over-reach Can be Misleading"; (b) "Pendleton Round-Up"; (c) *Hoss Trades.* In *H. Tradin'* as "Mine Mules."

No. 9, November, 1960. (a) "The Olympic Horse Events Are a Pale Performance as Compared to the Horse Events of the Inter-Allied Army Games of 1919"; (b) *Hoss Trades.* In *H. Tradin'* as "Nubbin."

No. 10, December, 1960. (a) "The First Issue of *Tally Book* was Published February 4, 1960, *The Old Tally Book"*; (b) *Hoss Trades,* "A Christmas Hoss Trade." In *H. Tradin' as* "Angel"; (c) "The Meaning of Christmas Through the Years." Also published by Green as "A Christmas Greeting" in broadside form.

No. 11, January, 1961. (a) "Will He Carry Weight?"; (b) "Guest of the Month: "Editor's Note: It is our belief that true horsemen all over the world have a great common bond in their love of horses. . . . We take pleasure in presenting a great horse of some breed other than our own in each issue of *The Tally Book."* [Article discusses the Standardbred and Morgan Trotting Horse.]; (c) *Hoss Trades.* In *H. Tradin'* as "The Parson's Mare, Bessie"; (d) "Last Summer when I was inspecting horses at Afton, Wyo., huge Elkhorn Archway" [caption under photo, signed "Doc"].

No. 12, February, 1961. (a) "A Horse's Performance is Affected by His Vision"; (b) *Hoss Trades*. In *H. Tradin'* as "Traveling Mare."

No. 13, March, 1961. (a) *Hoss Trades*. In *H. Tradin'* as "Poor Heifers — The Judge — Wild Mules."

No. 14, April, 1961. (a) "The Long and Short of Pasterns"; (b) *Hoss Trades*. In *H. Tradin'* as "Cowboy Trades for a Wagon and Team."

No. 15, Summer, 1961 [changed to Quarterly issue]. (a) *Hoss Trades*. In *H. Tradin'* as "Gypsy Hoss Trade"; (b) "They Ain't but One Type Quarter Horse; The Others Are Imitations."

No. 16, Fall, 1961. (a) "Irregular Pattern of Bone Structure; A horse is only as sound as his weakest bone or joint"; (b) *Hoss Trades*. In *H. Tradin'* as "Maniac Mule."

No. 17, Winter, 1962. (a) *Hoss Trades*. In *H. Tradin'* as "Horse from Round Rock."

No. 18, Spring, 1962. Nothing by Green in this issue .

No. 19, Fall, 1962. Nothing by Green in this final issue. But the back cover contains an advertisement written by him for his book, *Horse Conformation [and] Hoss Trades of Yesteryear*. It reads, "I done wrote a book! Excuse me. I intended to say, 'I have written a book about horses.' Published by Ridglea Publications, P. O. Box 7342, Fort Worth."

From the collector's standpoint, a complete set of the nineteen issues of *The Tally Book* must be considered the greatest rarity. I know of only three complete sets in private hands, although there are no doubt a number of single issues in the hands of the fortunate original subscribers. According to Green, all the unsold issues were stacked by him in his chicken house at the Pioneer Stock Farm in Cumby, where the chickens, not to mention rain, mildew, mice, insects, and time itself, have taken their respective tolls on the paper.

So far as I can determine, no notice whatever was taken by the news media of the first or subsequent issues of *The Tally Book*. As Green himself said, in *How Come I Wrote a Book*, "I had never considered a magazine an essential part of the horse business nor of the horse registry, but after the constant harping of 'It's almost everybody wants a magazine,' we decided we needed a magazine for the membership to have a medium of exchange of ideas and a means of advertising their registered horses. At the board of directors meeting, the matter was discussed, and it was unanimously agreed that the registry should have a magazine, but nobody wanted the responsibility of editing or publishing it. In January of 1960 . . . I started the publication of *The Tally Book* . . . and we were getting other interesting material but almost no advertisement, and the magazine was next to a total expense.

"Naomi Hallum [now Mrs. Naomi Scott, of Fort Worth] had come to work for the registry and was a very capable secretary and had experience in the publishing field. Old friends of mine would come in the office in San Angelo and tell old horse tradin' experiences that they had had with me . . . that I hadn't been too proud of, and had neglected to tell. All this material seemed very interesting to my secretary, Na, and she insisted that we publish some of these in *The Tally Book*. By now [it] was losing so much money and I was so disinterested that I told her we weren't about to waste any money taking up space with them damned yarns even though they were true.

"A magazine . . . breaks into units of four pages. While working on the next issue, Na came into my office and told me that we had a page and a half of news and some racing results, but there were two and a half pages . . . that would be blank if I didn't think of something to put on them. I said, 'Sit down over there and I'll give you a story.'

"I dictated her the story of 'The Rock Crusher and the Mule' that had happened to me on the trade grounds in Mineral Wells way back in the late twenties. She cleaned the story up and I never saw it again until it was in print.

"We entitled this little masterpiece 'Hoss Trades of Yesteryear,' and for the next several issues until we quit the publication of *The Tally Book,* we carried a story of 'Hoss Trades of Yesteryear.' "

Although I have not been able to locate press comment on *The Tally Book,* I have come across an article on its parent organization, the International Quarter Horse Jockey Club. The following is quoted from the *West Texas Livestock Weekly* of April 16, 1959, a date almost a year prior to the establishment of *The Tally Book.*

The article, "Horses are Measured, 'Plumbed' for Registry in New Association," by Russell Drake, reads in part:

> San Angelo. — Early in March, when fellow West Texans were bracing themselves against raw, bone-chilling winds, Ben K. "Doc" Green crowded his squat, ample frame behind the wheel of a green station wagon and motored out to sunny Southern California.
>
> Doc, who looks as though he might have stepped from between the covers of *The Pickwick Papers* or *David Copperfield,* . . . paused on the Pacific sands only briefly before bustling away to premises of some fifty ranchers and horse breeders in eight western states who had requested inspection of their horse flesh for registry in the International Quarter Horse Jockey Club, a new breeders association of which Green is secretary-treasurer.
>
> The fledgling registry is attracting considerable and widespread attention, Doc says, although it's tiny in comparison with Amarillo's American Quarter Horse Association, the breed's chief registry.
>
> On his return from the far West, 25 days and 9,645 miles later, Doc had accepted into the club 50 of 170 horses he peered, squinted, probed at, and painstakingly measured for conformation. In the four months he's been registering horses in the IQHJC, Doc says he's passed on 600 of 2,100 stallions, mares and foals paraded before his view in 17 states. He says he presently has a backlog of 300 oaters waiting for inspection and expects registrations to swell to between 3,000 and 5,000 by 1961.

That's a far cry, of course, from . . . the AQHA's 155,000 quarter horses registered over the past twenty years. But wagging a dimpled forefinger at a visitor to his small cluttered hotel office here, manned by himself and a lone secretary, Doc confidently predicts, "We'll have our own futurity by 1961."

To some extent, Green's Quarter Horse Jockey Club has its origins in a controversy that has raged in Quarter Horse circles since the breed began gaining popularity as a racing animal. How much additional Thoroughbred blood is desirable in the modern quarter horse? Is any, for that matter? The question has been only partly resolved in AQHA.

To Doc Green, the answer is simple. "The only thing good about a Quarter Horse is the Thoroughbred blood he's carrying. We encourage the use of Thoroughbred blood as long as it's Quarter type." But poll a dozen other Quarter Horse men on this subject and you'll get as many answers.

Of the International Quarter Horse Jockey Club, B. F. Phillips, Dallas oilman and QH breeder, says, "I'm afraid it's going to be just a place for somebody to go that has gripes. We would be better off if we put our efforts into one association."

An opposite view is held by outspoken John D. Askew, Fayetteville, Arkansas, QH breeder. . . . He says he's all for more associations or other activity involving use of Quarter Horses. "I'm interested in both using and racing Quarter Horses. The more things we can get going the better the market will be." He has one hundred Quarter Horses, all registered in AQHA, he says, and not long ago registered six mares with IQHJC.

To remove any doubt in his mind about a horse's qualifications and to "eliminate personalities" that might be involved . . . Doc Green employs a method of measuring and diagramming physical characteristics of a horse only slightly less exacting than a construction engineer might use to calculate erection of a suspension bridge. The system involves computing a maze of relationships between various portions of a horse's anatomy. A self-styled "student of the horse industry," Doc brings to the task a tape measure, plumb bob and a fund of knowledge gained from a life's experience with horses. . . .

"The girth is a horse's most important measurement," says Doc . . . "because the girth determines the heart and lung capacity. If you've got it you have a motor. If you haven't, you haven't got a motor."

⊄ 2 A. "The Meaning of Christmas—Through the Years." (First version, 1960.) One page, 8½ by 11 inches. Christmas greeting written by Green and sent to friends and customers. Printed in green ink on heavy eggshell finish paper, with a correction, "or" for "of" by pen in line three of the fifth paragraph. A greeting at the bottom in heavy type reads, "May all your stock have feed and shelter and you and yours a Joyous Christmas and a Bountiful New Year." Signed in print, "Ben K. Green." In all copies observed Green has signed his name in ink above the printed signature.

B. "The Meaning of Christmas—Through the Years." (A later version, no date). Printed on lighter weight paper, with minor changes in the wording of the text. The next to last line of the final paragraph of the text contains the misspelling "misstakes," and the greeting at the bottom has been revised to read, "May your camp be warm and safe and all your stock have feed and shelter, and may you and yours have a joyful Christmas and a bountiful New Year." Here Green's printed signature has been replaced by his "syringe G" brand at bottom right. In the lower left corner appears a drawing of an old-fashioned couple riding in a sleigh drawn by two horses.

In the text of these greetings, Green traces the development of his feelings about the meaning of Christmas from childhood, boyhood, young manhood, through older middle age. Here he becomes almost sentimental. "Now Christmas is the time that I miss my old friends who have ridden on since last Christmas to be gathered unto their fathers . . . to dwell

THE MEANING OF CHRISTMAS

Through the Years

The Christian meaning and the importance of Christmas was instilled into me at a very early age. However, all of this teaching was quickly overshadowed when I was a little boy by the goodies I could taste and the toys I could get my hands on and to me Christmas meant Santa Claus, fireworks and going to Greendaddy's (that was what I called my grandfather) for more goodies and more presents from more kinfolks.

When I was of school age Christmas meant gifts that I had hoped for a long time and Christmas meant parties, fun and visitors from near and far who came to bountiful feasts for days and days.

When I grew to be a young man I had already become a drifter and Christmas meant going home, big social affairs and meeting my former schoolmates and we outbragged each other about where we had been and what we had done since we saw each other last. I always told the good 'stay at home' boys what was over on the other side of the hill and how the trail was from here to there.

A few years later I took Christmas to count my blessings and invoice my worldly gatherings since last Christmas. I also wanted to make sure I got full credit from my friends and family for all my achievements too.

Now Christmas is the time that I miss my old friends who have ridden on since last Christmas to be gathered unto their fathers who have already made camp in green pastures by sparkling clear waters; no more to ride herd during drouth, blizzard and flood; to dwell in a place where their favorite horses will never be tired or grow old. At Christmas I think of the many new friends I have made whose acquaintance will enrich the years to come and I realize too that many people I had thought my enemies have proven to be friends I had misunderstood. I fondly remember the good times the year has brought and the good horses I have seen. I know that now I have gained a better meaning of Christmas because I fail to worry about recognition of my trivial successes. Instead I ponder what I have done or said and I wonder if I have at all times been fair to my fellow man. When I stop to realize how charitable people have been with me for my shortcomings and how forgiving for my many misstakes and the limitless praise I have received for my small efforts, it is with a feeling of humble gratitude that I sincerely extend my Christmas Greetings.

MAY YOUR CAMP BE WARM AND SAFE AND ALL YOUR STOCK HAVE FEED AND SHELTER AND MAY YOU AND YOURS HAVE A JOYFUL CHRISTMAS AND A BOUNTIFUL NEW YEAR.

The Meaning of Christmas—broadside B

in a place where their favorite horses will never be tired or grow old. At Christmas I think of the many new friends I have made . . . and that many people I had thought my enemies have proven to be friends I had misunderstood. I fondly remember the good times the year has brought and the good horses I have seen. I have gained a better meaning of Christmas because I fail to worry about recognition of my trivial successes. Instead I ponder what I have done or said and I wonder if I have at all times been fair to my fellow man. When I stop to realize how charitable people have been with me for my shortcomings and how forgiving for my many mistakes, and the limitless praise I have received for my small efforts, it is with a feeling of humble gratitude that I sincerely extend my Christmas Greetings. Ben K. Green."

A rare insight, indeed, to an even rarer humility!

¶ 3 *Horse Conformation* [*and*] *Hoss Trades of Yesteryear* Privately published, Fort Worth, 1963. 141 pp., text in double columns, hardback in black plastic-coated cloth, black dust jacket printed in green and white. Stamping on the spine and front cover is in imitation gold, usually turning green. There is no title page; the information usually found thereon must be gleaned from the stamping on the front cover and spine of the book, and from the somewhat differing versions printed on the front and spine of the dust jacket. The wording of the eight lines on the front cover is arranged as follows:

HORSE CONFORMATION
As to Soundness And
Performance Ability
and
HOSS TRADES OF YESTERYEAR

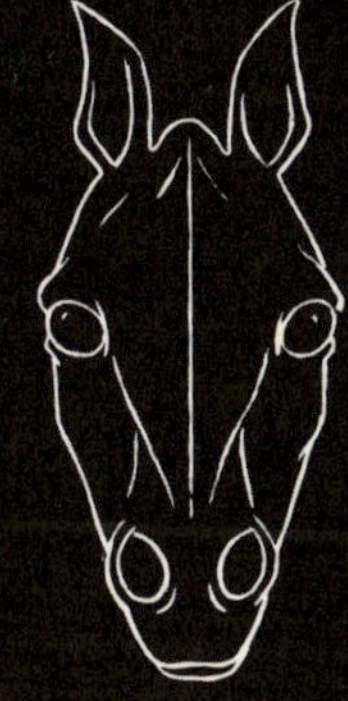

Horse Conformation and Hoss Trades of Yesterday—dust jacket

Written and Published
By
Ben K. Green

The arrangement of the wording on the front of the dust jacket is as follows:

HORSE
CONFORMATION
As to
Soundness — Performance — Ability
[Outline of Horse Face]
HOSS TRADES
Of Yesteryear

The wording stamped vertically along the spine of the book reads simply:

HORSE CONFIRMATION and
HOSS TRADES OF YESTERYEAR

while that on the spine of the dust jacket reads:

First Edition HORSE CONFORMATION Ben K. Green

The copyright page immediately follows the blank free endpaper, and contains the following information:

Copyright, 1963
By BEN K. GREEN
Pioneer Stock Farm
All rights reserved, including
the right to reproduce this book
or portions thereof in any form.
First Edition
Composition by Naomi Hallum

The verso of the copyright page contains Green's five paragraph Foreword, in which he demonstrates an ability to write the English language in clear non-vernacular prose. For example: "The primary purpose of this book is to emphasize and illustrate the horse as an animal of living, mechanical perfection. The principles of mechanics, leverage, and the natural law of physics were not invented by man, and were not first brought to civilization in the form of steel and other metals formed into man-made contraptions."

"Horse Conformation" occupies the first sixty-six pages of the book. It contains sixteen short chapters, reprinted, with their illustrations, from *The Tally Book*. The chapters deal with "Heads," "Vision," "The Neck," "The Spine," "The Thorax," "Shoulders," "Forelegs," "Pasterns," "Hindquarters," "Hocks," "Feet," "Irregular Pattern of Bone Structure," "Will He Carry Weight?," "The Top Line," "Stride," and "The 'Forward Seat.' "

In these chapters the anatomical details are discussed in terms of their effect upon the animal's suitability to the work for which its owner acquired it, whether for racing, polo, drayage, farm plowing, breeding, trotting, or showing.

Pages [67] and [68] are blank. *Hoss Trades of Yesteryear* begins on the page numbered 69, which contains a brief introduction, and serves as the only title page to the stories. It reads as follows:

HOSS TRADES OF YESTERYEAR

"I claim to be one of the few men left this side of 'walkin' cane age' who took advantage of early educational opportunities around wagon yards, livery stables, and mule barns, which has afforded me a genuine wagon-yard background.

"No modern day horseman will ever have the opportunity to gain such inside knowledge of the horse business, since the passing of these old institutions.

> "These 'Hoss Trades of Yesteryear' are retold just as they occurred during my early years of experiences as a horse trader. Nothing has been added or left out in order to put varnish on them for modern day reading.
>
> "It is my hope that they will add to your reading pleasure, and possibly cause many of you to reminisce of some humorous incidents that may have occurred to you in your experiences with horses and horse traders."

This wording differs slightly from the introductory paragraph heading the "Hoss Trades" stories in *The Tally Book,* which contained an additional sentence reading, "The following incident is just one of the many 'short courses' in horsemanship taught to me by the old masters of the trade."

Page 70 is not numbered and is blank. Beginning on page 71 the book reprints, without change, the fifteen stories previously published in the issues of *The Tally Book*. Here for the first time the stories are given individual titles: "Gypsy Hoss Trade," "Homer's Last Mule" (listed in the table of contents as "Homer's *'Latest'* Mule"), "Nubbin," "Angel," "Maniac Mule," "Matched Mares," "The Rock Crusher and the Mule," "A Road Horse for a Broodmare," "Cowboy Trades for a Wagon n' Team," "Poor Heifers — The Judge-Wild Mules," "The Parson's Mare, Bessie," "Horse from Round Rock," "Mule Colts," "Mine Mules," and "Traveling Mare." Green then adds a new story, *not* published in *The Tally Book,* entitled "The School Marm and Ol' Nothin'," and a final article (on pages 140–141) headed "Trend of Horse Population," which, he explains, "is included in this book because of its historical value . . . for study and comparison in the breeding of horses in the years to come."

Green tells of his experience in publishing and marketing *Horse Conformation* [*and*] *Hoss Trades of Yesteryear* in *How Come I Wrote a Book*.

> "We had a Varitype machine in the office that was used to make all the composition for *The Tally Book* and Na had made the composition and layout for the book in such a manner that it could be printed without any typesetting expense. After making some inquiries, I went to Dallas and had an agricultural printing company . . . to print a thousand copies of my book. There was something the matter with the machine at the bindery and some blank pages showed up in 56 of the books. This left 944 good copies.
>
> "This is when I began to learn about the publishing business. An unknown individual can do almost nothing with his own book. I didn't know how to sell it, how to get it reviewed or publicize it. . . . It was priced at $7.50 retail and I sold it for $5.00 when I found a sucker that would buy a copy. I carried them in my car, had some on my desk in my office, and most of the time carried one in my coat pocket with the title showing, hoping somebody would ask about it. There were a few people I think bought it out of pity for me and occasionally I swapped a few copies for gas at a filling station where there would be some cowboy working.
>
> "After a couple of years, I still had over half of these little jewels, didn't near have my money back, and had about quit making any effort to sell them. . . . Now, since I have finally been recognized as a genius (modest as I am) and this was my first published book, collectors have paid all the way from $25 to $125 for this original."

Green stored the unsold copies of his jewel in the chicken house of his "batchin' shack" in Cumby, where, like the unsold copies of *The Tally Book,* they lay watersoaked and moulding for several years. Thus copies in good to fine condition, with dust jacket, are very scarce, and on the rare book market bring as much as $250 for a single copy. I recall the day he came into my shop with one of them in his hand, after he had become famous. I said, "Ben, what do you want for that old black book of yours?"

He replied, "Well, old so-and-so just paid me $125 for a

copy not as good as this one. Now I know you got to make a livin', so you can have this one for only $100."

I acted stunned and hurt. "Ben," I said, "the last time you were in here you sold me two copies at $45 apiece. What's the idea?"

"Hell, there ain't no more of these. I got this copy from one of my old school teachers that I had given two copies to, just to show her I was smart enough to write a book. And I'm about out of old school teachers."

There was more argument on my part, but an ex-lawyer bookseller is no match for an old horse trader, and I wound up paying him the $100, on condition that he would inscribe the volume "This is a first edition of my first book, Ben K. Green." He was happy to do this, since it didn't cost him anything, and I was happy to call up a customer who collected Green's books, and he in turn was happy to add it to his collection at a reasonable charge over the amount I had paid. So everybody was happy.

BOOK REVIEW OF HORSE CONFORMATION

The American West Review, December 1, 1967, vol. 1, no. 4. Review entitled "Ben K. Green: Swami of the Sacred Swap," by Owen Ulph, at that time a contributing editor of *The American West,* and Professor of Humanities at Reed College, Portland, Oregon. Joint review of *Horse Conformation* (the first hard-back edition) and *Horse Tradin'*. Concerning *Horse Conformation* the reviewer says, in part:

"*Horse Conformation* should be required reading for everyone who, at any time in his life, has climbed on a horse's back or contemplates doing so. From it he will learn that there are a lot of habits often regarded as manifestations of orneriness . . . that are attributable to the structure of their anatomy—such as balking, boogering, shying, snorting, spooking, forging, and side-winding. A careful reading of Green's book should make a better rider and a better man."

"*Horse Conformation* belongs on a shelf with Walton's *Compleat Angler,* Burton's *Anatomy of Melancholy,* Mrs. Beeton's *Cookery and Household Management,* and Stendahl's *De L'Amour*. My immediate reaction after finishing it was that everything else ever written about the horse — including my own inspired observations, but excluding Xenophon's *On Equitation* — could be thrown away. I even indulged in fantasies of running Green for President and giving Texas a chance to redeem itself."

❡ 4 "*How to Tell the True Age of a Horse by the Teeth / From 6 Months to 29 Years Old.*" This is a large wall poster, measuring 4 feet 10 inches in width by 3 feet 6 inches in height. It contains forty-five illustrations of horses' teeth at various ages, reproduced by Green from the woodcut pictures in an unidentifiable old textbook on horses, with a legend under each illustration written by him. In the lower right-hand corner there is a picture of a smiling somewhat baby-faced Green, to the right of which appears the printed notice: "Copies of this chart / can be ordered from / Dr. Ben K. Green, / Pioneer Stock Farm, / Cumby, Texas / Price $5.00 Post Paid / Copyright 1963."

The pictures and text of the poster were used, in reduced form, in the last chapters of the first and second pamphlet editions of *Horse Conformation as to Soundness and Performance,* and as illustrations numbered 59 to 90 in Northland's hardback edition of that work.

The poster was apparently designed to be sold to riding stables and horse barns, and to be used as a visual aid in the lectures Green often gave before riding club groups.

❡ 5 "Gray Mules: A Reminiscence." *Southwest Review,* Summer, 1965, vol. L, no. 3, pp. 253–69. Southern Methodist

University Press, Dallas, Texas, 1965. Fiftieth Anniversary Issue.

The story, later reprinted in *Horse Tradin'* as "The Gray Mules," tells how Green traded a pair of unmanageable draft horses for a beautifully dappled team of gray mules. When a rainstorm washes the fine youthful color from their coats, leaving them an aging white, Green resolves to find a way to trade them back to the seller and get even, learning one of the tricks of the trade in the process.

According to Green's account in *How Come I Wrote a Book,* he was pressured into writing "Gray Mules." He says:

> I . . . had forgot about my literary career when the editor of *The Southwest Review,* in the company of an old girlfriend of mine, came into my office in Greenville, Texas. They had made the trip [from Dallas] for the sole purpose of having me write a story for *The Southwest Review* but I wasn't interested in writing a story for it or any other publication. However, after several set-tos and harassments, I consented to write the story "The Grey [*sic*] Mules" which appeared in *The Southwest Review* Summer 1965 issue, a quarterly publication of the SMU Press.

But according to Margaret Hartley, then and now the editor of the *Southwest Review,* Green came to *her* office on the SMU campus in Dallas, accompanied by a young woman, a friend of Ms. Hartley's, who typed the manuscript of "Gray Mules" from a dictating machine recording made by Green. The young lady and her family had been friends of Green's family when she was a little girl. She was in no sense "an old girlfriend." There was no trip to Greenville, there were no "set-tos and harassments," and Green accepted $40 in payment for the story, at the then going rate for contributions.

Whatever the circumstances surrounding its origin, however, the appearance of "Gray Mules" in the prestigious *Southwest Review,* which boasted among its stable of contributors

Gray Mules: A Reminiscence

BEN K. GREEN

ONE WINTER I was feeding a bunch of steers on the Brazos River on a big old rough ranch—rough pasture and lots of canyons and draws. The river was winding, and it was a hard kind of country to get your feed out into the pasture to feed cattle. Of course, in those days, we used wagons and teams for everything.

I had a young team of horses that were thrown in on the deal when I leased the ranch, and that were supposed to be unbroke. Well, that was putting it mildly. Generally when you say a team is unbroke, you are talking about young horses three or four or five years old that just never have been worked. When I got this team up, they were a pair of well-matched bay, bald-faced horses that weighed about fourteen hundred, and instead of being four or five years old and unbroke—they were eight or nine years old and had been broke *at*. But there was sure nobody had ever done much of a job of breaking them.

They were the rankest, big draft-type horses that I had ever had any experience with. When you roped them, they choked and pawed and fought. Then when you got them up and got your hands on them, you would have to tie a foot up on each one to harness them—if you didn't, they would kick you from behind and paw you in front and bite you anytime you weren't looking. Generally, big horses are gentle, but these weren't.

Every morning after I'd load my feed wagon, I'd start to hitch up this team. That meant I'd have to rope them and tie them to a tree and try to get harness on them. And after I'd get them harnessed—each one separately—I'd have to get them up by the side of each other and hook them together and then run them over the wagon tongue—two or three times—before I ever got them to stop where I could draw them back in position to hook them to the wagon. After

"Grey Mules: A Reminiscence" in *Southwest Review*

such literary luminaries as J. Frank Dobie, Frieda Lawrence, Paul Horgan, Henry Miller, Walter Prescott Webb, and Mabel Dodge Luhan, marked a turning point in Green's career. It was the first publication of his writings not paid for and distributed by himself — indeed, it was the first for which he received payment as an author; it precipitated him, willy nilly, into the world of the *literati,* a world he affected to disdain; it preceded his first nationally published book, *Horse Tradin',* by nearly two years; and, most importantly for his career as a writer, the story happened to be read and savored by Ashbel Greene, a senior editor for publisher Alfred A. Knopf. In *How Come I Wrote a Book* Doc Green explains the occurrence:

> Ash Greene . . . happened to pick up this quarterly and read "Gray Mules; A Reminiscence." He called this story to the attention of Angus Cameron, who is editor-in-chief at Knopf. It is my understanding that this part of the country [i.e., the Southwest] and this kind of material came under his jurisdiction. He wrote me a letter telling me who he was and he would like for me to write a book of these stories to be published by Alfred A. Knopf, Inc. This letter didn't excite me too much since I had already had some expensive experience in the writing business and had decided that I was a better horse inspector and horse trader than I was a writer.

Nevertheless, when he found out that the publisher would actually pay him a substantial cash sum in advance, he decided that he was not such a bad writer after all, and went to work on the manuscript of *Horse Tradin'.*

REVIEW OF GRAY MULES

Southwest Review, Summer, 1965, vol. L, no. 3, beginning on preliminary page v. So far as I am able to determine, the following remarks, (although not a book review in the usual sense) represent the *first* description of Ben K. Green as an author of books, as distinguished from the veterinarian. Ms. Margaret Hartley is the writer, and she lists the following biographical data from Green, himself:

"With Ben K. Green's 'Gray Mules: A Reminiscence,' we introduce a Texan who is, we think, squarely in the tradition of great Texas storytellers. All of Ben Green's stories come, as does this one, from his own experience. He is a man who unites a compendious memory with a wryly humorous and affectionate understanding of the nature of such animals as horses, cattle, and human beings. He is a native of Cumby, a small town near Greenville, Texas. The name is no coincidence; he belongs to one of the four Green families who settled in Greenville (originally Greensville) before it became a town. He has a right to the title of Texan from way back; his grandmother was the first white child born in the area that is now Hopkins and Hunt counties. When he was twelve he left home on horseback for Weatherford, Texas, and though after that his range extended over almost the whole world, the horses and cattle of the Southwest have remained the real focus of his life.

"He studied veterinary medicine at Cornell, with postgraduate work in England and Australia. At one time he traveled over most of the civilized world (with the exception of Russia, China, and Japan) on a foundation-supported soil and plant survey, concentrating on his specialty of botanical toxicology. He has also practiced veterinary medicine in the far Southwest, along the Pecos and the Rio Grande, in one of the last big 'horse countries' of North America. He has never lost his delight in the sort of horse-trading escapade he describes in 'Gray Mules.' Now, back in Cumby, he is raising the small red Devon cattle he saw and appreciated in England."

¶ 6 *Diagram to Show the Construction and Proportions of a Good Horse's Forelegs and Hindlegs — Made After Reading Horse Conformation by Ben K. Green.* Tom Lea, 1966.

Broadside, quarto (11 by 14 inches), 1-page, on stiff paper, printed by Carl Hertzog, El Paso, Texas, in an edition of 100 copies. The broadside depicts a front view and a rear view of a horse, the front view being taken from Illustration E on page 27 of Green's *Horse Conformation* [*and*] *Hoss Trades of Yesteryear,* and the rear view from Illustration B on page 35 of that book. Lea has superimposed his own cross-hatching lines and shaded backgrounds on the drawings, providing, in effect, an "architect's rendering" of the proportions of the horse. He has handlettered the title beneath the pictures. Green used the Lea drawings, much reduced in size, on the front covers of his pamphlet editions of *Horse Conformation as to Soundness and Performance,* published in 1969 and 1972, respectively. They do not appear in either the trade or limited editions of this work, republished by Northland Press in 1975 in handsome hardback volumes.

[Compiler's note]: It seems a pity that two such talented artists in their respective mediums — Lea in painting and Green in personal reminiscence — should not have been able to get together on one of their common interests, good horses. Green told me that he had seen a copy of this drawing of Lea's, and he thought Lea might be interested in doing the illustrations for *Horse Tradin',* to be published by Knopf. He approached Lea through Carl Hertzog, Lea's friend and fellow townsman, but Lea refused to see him, claiming he was too busy with other matters.

This made Green mad, and not being one to relinquish a good grudge, he thereafter remained critical of Lea's horse paintings. On one of his visits to the bookshop the subject of horse paintings came up (as it was likely to do when Green was around) and after a few derogatory remarks he asked for a copy of *The Hands of Cantú,* Lea's classic story developed around a legendary Spanish horse trainer of Old Mexico. Turning to a picture of a rearing horse on page [146] Green remarked, with some heat: "That isn't a real horse; in two seconds that horse would be falling on its nose, and the rider would be sailing through the air!"

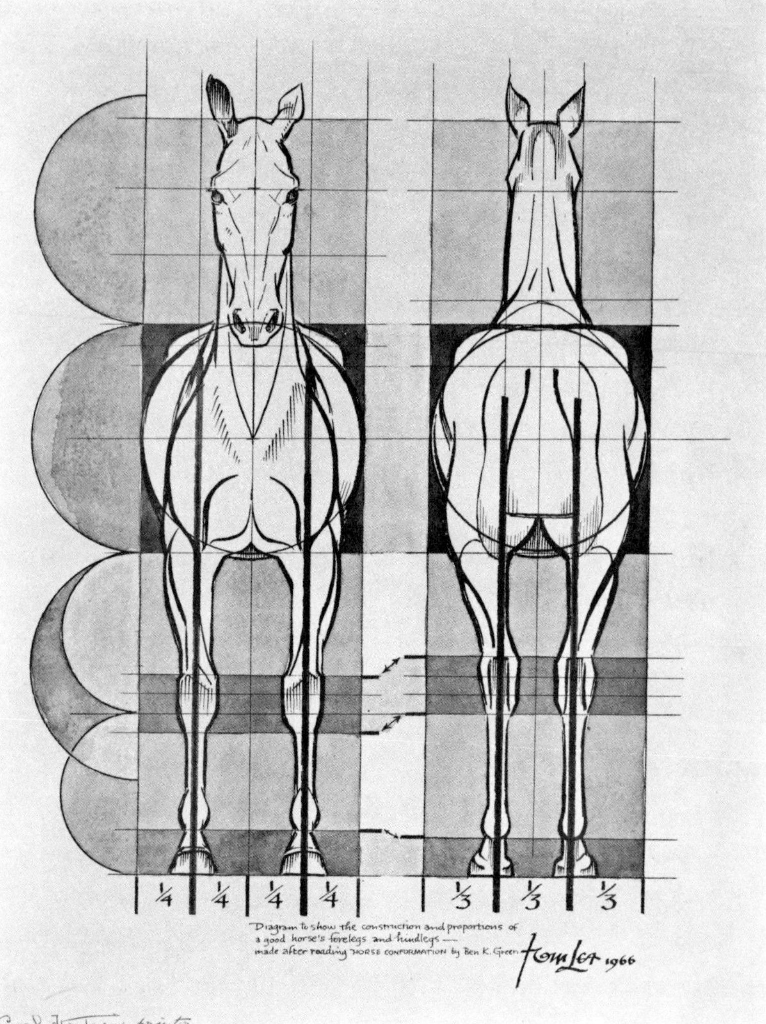

Tom Lea broadside on *Horse Conformation*

Perhaps it was hardly to be expected that Ben Green (who had, as one newsman expressed it, "the personality of a cuckle-bur") and Tom Lea, with his *hurañería,* should hit it off together on a book. But what a combination it might have made!

The scarcity of this broadside (only 100 copies of the original), together with the combination of Tom Lea's drawing, Carl Hertzog's printing, and Green's horse expertise, have made it a much-sought collector's item.

¶ 7 *Horse Tradin'*. (Published only in the regular or trade editions). Horse Tradin' / by Ben K. Green / Illustrations by Lorence Bjorklund / Alfred A. Knopf / [Borzoi dog insert] New York. 1967.

Octavo (8½ by 6 inches), 304 pp., plus pp. [305] and [306]. The binding of the first edition, and subsequent printings through the thirteenth, was in black cloth covers, with "Horse Tradin' " stamped in blind (i.e., *not* gold-stamped) within an oval panel on the front cover, and Knopf's "Borzoi Books" dog blind-stamped at the bottom right of the rear cover. The spine was of light cream-colored linen, with the title, author, and publisher's name printed in dark brown ink sometimes found faded or worn to a lighter brown in some copies of the first or early editions. The binding of the *fourteenth* printing (in March, 1975, according to its copyright page) was entirely in cream-colored linen, without the black cloth covers.

The collation of the first edition is as follows: The front free endpaper is blank on both sides. Page [i] is the half-title, reading simply "Horse Tradin'." Page [ii] forms the left half of a double-spread title page and contains a pencil drawing of four horses by Bjorklund which extends across the "gutter,"

Angel

One summer I was traveling the far Southwest. It had been a long, hot day, and I had crossed the desert of lower Arizona and New Mexico and driven into Albuquerque. I hadn't stopped to eat lunch, and it was middle afternoon, so I walked into a hotel coffee shop and sat down at the counter. There were people at a few tables and a few stragglers like me at the counter, but it was far from a busy place. I looked at the menu, and it looked like the last few thousand I had read, so I ordered something and ate it from force of habit. Really, I guess I was enjoying the air conditioning and the rest from the road more than the food. I got up from the counter and walked toward

Horse Tradin'—Lorence Bjorklund illustration on page 62

or inner hinge, to page [iii] the title page proper, reading as above. Page [iv], the copyright page, contains information reading in part as follows: "This is a Borzoi Book / . . . First Edition / Copyright 1963, 1965, 1967 by Ben K. Green / . . . The chapter 'Gray Mules' appeared in the July 1965 / issue of *Southwest Review.* / The following chapters appeared in / *Horse Conformation* by Ben K. Green: [Here follow the titles of sixteen stories, out of the twenty in the book, published in *Horse Conformation — Hoss Trades of Yesteryear.*] Preliminary pages v through xi contain Green's preface, a short account of the organization of the horse and mule business before the coming of the internal combustion engine. Page [xii] is blank. Pages xiii and xiv hold the table of contents. [1] is the half-title, reading simply *Horse Tradin';* [2] is blank except for Bjorklund's pencil drawing of a recumbent horse, which extends across to page [3] where the text begins. Pages numbered 4 through 304 contain the text. At the end of the book page [305] contains "A Note about the Author," and page [306] "A Note on the Type."

"A Note about the Author" on page [305], seventeen lines printed in italics, includes the following statement: "He studied veterinary medicine at Cornell University and did post-graduate work at the Royal College of Veterinary Medicine in England — Dr. Green has done subsequent research on toxic plant life, etc." — a statement requiring, or at least inviting, further comment hereinafter.

The dust jacket is printed in black and orange-red on buff paper, with a Bjorklund pencil drawing of a man examining a horse's teeth occupying nearly half of the front cover. The author's name is given as "Ben K. Green, D.V.M." [i.e., Doctor of Veterinary Medicine]. A brief biographical sketch on the rear flap of the jacket repeats the statement of "A Note about the Author" that Green "studied veterinary medicine at Cornell University and did postgraduate work at the Royal College of Veterinary Medicine in England."

Now those who have taken the trouble to investigate Green's claims to an impressive educational background report that neither Cornell University nor "The Royal College of Veterinary Medicine" has any record of the attendance of anyone named Ben King Green, leading to the conclusion, or at least to the probability, that Green's oft-repeated designation of himself as "Doctor" Green, and the use of the letters D.V.M. denoting possession of a doctor's degree in veterinary medicine, were apocryphal and self-bestowed, somewhat in the tradition of the old-time "Southern Colonels." It may or may not be significant, moreover, that no diplomas or other evidences of academic achievement beyond high school level have as yet been found among his personal papers. This fact, of course, is not conclusive; he was by his own admission careless in record keeping, and indifferent to, if not actually contemptuous of, academic qualificatons (aside from claiming them himself). He was always on the move during his practice as a veterinarian, and it would not be surprising if his diplomas (if he had any) should have become lost somewhere along the course of a busy and roving life.

From the bibliographic viewpoint it is interesting to note that all references to Green's study at Cornell and postgraduate work in England were eliminated (one knowledgeable authority says at Green's own request) from the rear flap of the dust jackets of the second printing and all subsequent printings; the revised statement reads, "He studied veterinary medicine in the United States and abroad, and practiced in the Far Southwest. . . ." But strangely, no such revision has been made in the text of "A Note about the Author" on page [305] in the book, and all editions including the latest, still credit him with study at Cornell and the Royal College of Veterinary Medicine, even though for the fourteenth printing (in 1975) the "Note about the Author" was revised (as was the biographical sketch on the dust jacket) to note Green's death late in 1974, offering an opportunity to eliminate the apocryphal academic credits. And somehow, the author of *Horse Tradin'* is still "Ben K. Green, D.V.M." on all versions of the dust jacket.

Two other points deserve consideration in this connection. The first is that nowhere in his writings does Green *himself* claim to have attended Cornell or the Royal College; the claims are made in statements written by the publisher's people — based, undoubtedly, on information furnished orally by Green himself. Secondly, the claims appear only in *Horse Tradin'*, but in none of his later books, a circumstance indicating that he was not inclined to make a point of the matter.

In the final analysis, Green's appropriation of an educational background he did not have would affect his credibility, and hence his acceptance as a competent veterinarian by others of that profession. His writings in the field of veterinary science, especially in the fields of toxicology and the color of horses, must stand on their own merits, and be damned, praised, or ignored by the experts, as is the custom in professional circles.

But in the profession of literary story-telling, as in politics or horse trading, an author's truthfulness is not at so high a premium, and may even be a liability to him. In Green's case, the delightful stories in *Horse Tradin'* and his later books, dealing with his adventures with the animals and men of rural America, have preserved the colorful heritage of a time we shall never see again. A whole string of academic degrees or scholarly honors after his name would not enhance our enjoyment in reading them.

Finally, as a commentary on the progress of inflation, the

price of the book is listed on the first edition dust jacket at \$5.95; on later printings at \$6.95, and on the fourteenth printing at \$7.95. And as a further commentary on the appreciation in value of good books, collectors are now willing to pay \$50.00 and up for fine copies of the first edition of *Horse Tradin'* in the original dust jacket. What they will have to pay five years from now is anybody's guess.

BOOK REVIEWS OF HORSE TRADIN'

The New York Times Book Section, June 11, 1967. Book review entitled "Beware the Snide," by Fred Gipson.

The first edition of *Horse Tradin'* was published on May 22, 1967. On the second Sunday following, there appeared what must be considered the most important — if not the first — nation-wide press notice in Green's writing career, a seventy-three-line review of his book in the prestigious *New York Times* Book Section, and by no less a reviewer than the late internationally famed Fred Gipson, author of *Hound Dog Man, Old Yeller, Savage Sam, Fabulous Empire,* and other best-sellers.

The review's primacy in chronology, authorship, and source entitles it to more than usual quotation in this bibliography. Gipson writes:

"The time is the 1930s, when money was a scarce commodity and automobiles and farm tractors were just beginning to replace horses and mules as a means of motive power. Horse lover that he was, young Green owned an automobile. The impression he wanted to make was that of being 'a big operator from out West' who was just passing through, but who might be interested in trading for a few horses or mules, if the price were right. He dressed the part and talked the part; and generally, somewhere in Texas, New Mexico, Mississippi or Oklahoma, he could run onto a deal. It might be with a sharp gypsy trader, a dignified old Southern colonel, a soul-saving man of God, or some poor farmer down on his luck and forced to sell — but all were out to 'skin' him. Every now and then they did. . . . But having received no mercy, young Green gave none. When he got a chance to turn one of his snides, he didn't let his conscience get in the way of making a profit — if he could — and often he did.

. . . Mr. Green handles his subject matter with the same quiet ease and confidence with which he obviously went about taming a wild mule."

The Knickerbocker News, Albany, New York, June 11, 1967. Book review entitled "Tales of a Horse Trader," reviewed by Duane LaFleche under the heading "Books & Authors." This review, appearing on the same date as that of Gipson in the *New York Times,* was considerably longer and more detailed, with quotations from the stories: particularly "Easter Lily." The reviewer concludes: "There is in all these stories a certain gentility, a kind of country courtesy and the refreshing remembrances of hard work in hard times that make them a welcome relief from much of the inward-struggle, psychological twaddle, sex-saturated stuff we get to read nowadays."

Fort Worth Star-Telegram, June 11, 1967. Review entitled " 'Hoss Trades' Recall Era," by Leonard Sanders. The reviewer notes in passing that *Horse Tradin'* "is scheduled for publication Monday," which would make the publication date June 12, 1967, rather than May 22, as stated by Knopf on the copyright page of later editions. The review continues: "The book, expanded from an earlier, privately printed volume, *Horse* [*sic*] *Trades of Yesteryear,* may well become a classic akin to Andy Adams's *The Log of a Cowboy,* and it is certainly a leading contender for whatever Texana awards are handed out this year. Its success is assured; before formal publication it has gone into a second printing. A natural story teller, [Green] is a keen observer with virtually total recall. He remembers not only the personalities of the people involved in his experiences, but also the personalities of the horses and mules."

The National Observer, Princeton, N.J., July 3, 1967. Review entitled "A Horse Swapper Recalls the Days of Trading Tricks." "Mr. Green writes as a man might talk in the company of good friends who are in no hurry, letting one yarn build up to the point he'd planned to make."

San Angelo [Texas] *Times,* July 23, 1967: Review entitled "Old Time Horse Traders Not Exactly Trustworthy," by Elmer Kelton. "Ranchmen all over Texas know Ben K. (Doc) Green, who practiced veterinary medicine and lived in San Angelo many years before moving to the Fort Worth area. Green has been famed among his acquaintances as a gifted yarn spinner. For hours on end he would hold sway over a bemused hotel-lobby audience, telling of his horse-trading years. . . .

"Having known Doc Green some twenty years, this reviewer is not going to take the stand and swear that every story is one-hundred per cent true as written. But they are all told the way they should have happened, at least. When you've finished it, you may not want to buy a horse from him, but you'll probably be ready to buy another book."

Lawton [Oklahoma] *Constitution-Press,* June 15, 1967. Review entitled "Horse Tradin' Yarns Charm Readers; Funny Stories of What West Was and Is," by Paul McClung, in "Books in Review."

Dallas Times Herald, 1967. Review entitled "Immediate Artistry of Ben Green," by A. C. Greene, Book Editor, in "The Printed Page." "A great many of today's writers have never been anything but writers. For sure, they may have worked at odd jobs along to keep them alive, they may have taught school or been on newspapers or loaded freighters for a summer . . . but their life view has always been that of the writer, the outsider watching the insiders work and play and make fools of themselves.

"Ben Green, on the other hand, took to writing only after he was satisfied with another career and saw in it the universalities of truth which writers must always find — or which sometimes find the writer in spite of himself. One must suppose this to be the case of Ben Green. I cannot believe this man self-consciously set out to become another Frank Dobie, say, or to compete, in his own mind, with other Texas pens. He is an original who could, and probably would, have written *Horse Tradin'* without having read or heard of Dobie. . . .

"Ben Green is like Dobie only in their ability to capture human nature and the essence of a regional society and translate them into terms and pictures we can relate to no matter what our own nature, region or society might be. But I must say this, as a personal tribute, that only John Graves' . . . 1960 *Goodbye to a River* . . . has captured me like my first reading of *Horse Tradin'*. The sheer entertainment value of his stories puts Ben Green, at once, in the master class."

Greenville [Texas] *Herald Banner,* August 20, 1967. This comes from a four-column review entitled "Ben Green's Folks Are Real," by James W. Byrd, in "Views and Previews." "What makes *Horse Tradin'* sell so well? I'm often asked. Well, you are interested in 'real folks,' and a lot of other readers are too. The folks in Ben's books are real."

The American West Review, December 1, 1967, p. 9. Review entitled "Ben K. Green: Swami of the Sacred Swap," by Owen Ulph. Although labeled as a review of *Horse Tradin',* the first part of Ulph's extended essay deals with Green's *Horse Conformation,* and his comments on the latter book are included in this bibliography under that title. With regard to *Horse Tradin'* he says, in part: "There is no way to do justice to Green's book except to read it. Anyone who has not yet enjoyed the experience is to be envied. . . . Green is a natural story teller, the type of writer who never needs to learn the rules because he is more than capable of making his own. His picaresque personality permeates every page — in form, construction, narrative technique, insight, manner, intrusions and asides. In other words, Green has *style.*

". . . *Horse Tradin'* is a morally uplifting book. The reader gradually expands in the grip of the beatific vision that all men are scoundrels with the taint of larceny in their souls and the revelation that the world should thank its sinners and not its saints for saving it from dullness. Gratitude can also be extended to the throng of horses and mules whose roguish personalities enliven the pages of the book and convey all sorts of illuminating philosophical and psychological messages."

¶ 8 *The Shield Mares.* 1967: The Encino Press: Austin. Ben K. Green: Introduction by A. C. Greene. Copyright 1967: Ben K. Green.

Thin octavo. 47 pp. The book is bound in boards, with a flat spine, the covering paper having the appearance of light tan marble. The front cover contains the outline of a shield in black, while the back cover contains Green's "brand," the out-

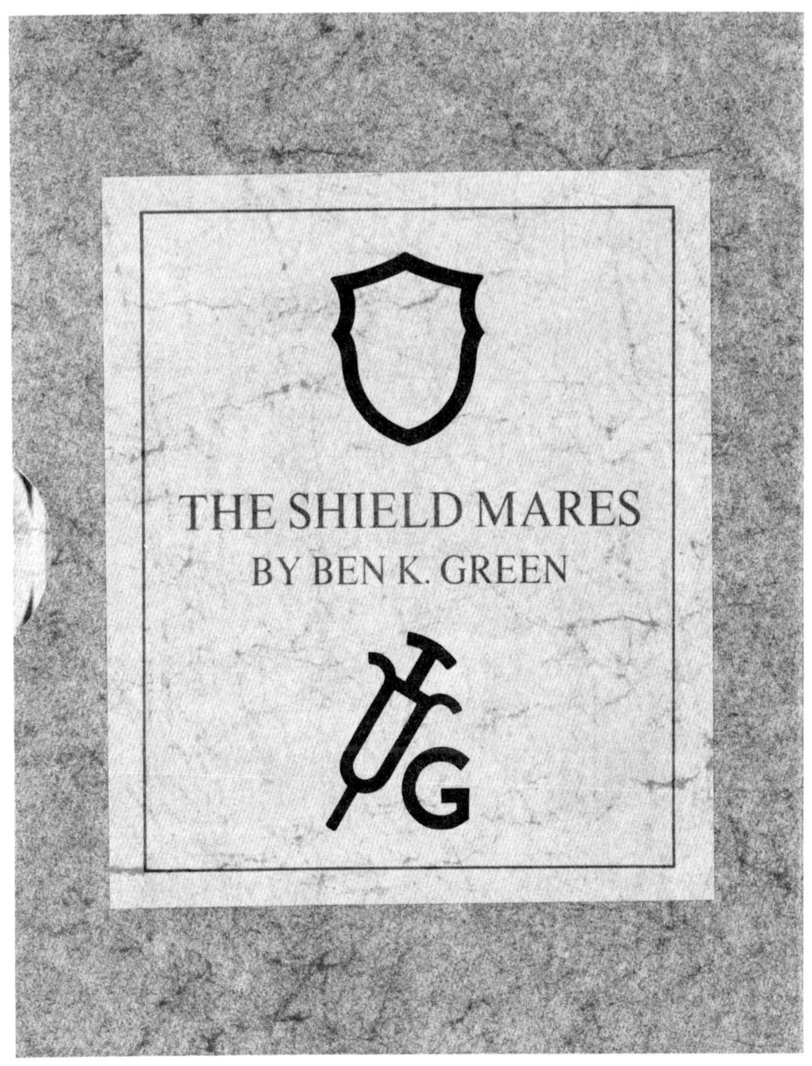

The Shield Mares in slipcase

line of a veterinary's syringe above a capital G. The title on the spine, printed horizontally in brown ink, reads; "Ben K. Green: The Shield Mares: The Encino Press."

Collation: the free endpaper, blank on both sides, is followed by a blank preliminary leaf bearing the signature "Ben K. Green" in ink. Preliminary pages [i–iv] contain the half-title, the double-page title, and the copyright page. A. C. Greene's Introduction occupies pages v through vii; the reverse of page vii is blank. Page [1] is a repetition of the half-title, with its verso blank. The text proper begins on numbered page 3, and continues without chapter breaks through page 47. Page [48] contains a colophon reading:

> 750 copies of THE SHIELD MARES, each signed by the author, have been published *con mucho gusto* by the Encino Press in September, 1967. No. ——. Printed by the Whitley Company from 12-point Times Roman . . . on Creme Blanc paper . . . and bound and slipcased by Custom Bookbindery according to the design by William D. Wittliff.

The light-weight cardboard slipcase is covered in a darker-toned marble paper, with a large title label printed on the same light-toned marble paper as the book covers.

This was Green's second commercially published and distributed book, being preceded only by *Horse Tradin'*, published some three months earlier.

Many critics, and perhaps most readers, consider *The Shield Mares* to be not only Green's best story, but one of the classic short stories of the Southwest. Having seen one or two fine horses bearing a brand in the form of a shield, Green determines to find the ranch from which they came, and, if possible, buy up the remainder of the herd. He finds the ranch in deep South Texas on the Mexican border, and learns that the remaining horses, all mares, are the pure-blooded descendants of a strain of Arabian steeds brought from Spain many years ago. He buys them, paying half the price down, with delivery to be made at the ranch corral on the following Monday. That night at supper in the little town of La Rio he befriends an elderly Mexican aristocrat on his way home to his rancheria in Mexico. The next morning this gentleman tells Green that he is about to be cheated; the Shield Mares have been trained to run away and hide in the rough canyon country before their purchaser can drive them to the main road. If he returns to the ranch to get his money back, he finds it deserted. With the Mexican as his mentor, Green plans a way to keep the horses from breaking loose. This scheme, plus the "O. Henry ending," make absorbing and delightful reading.

The scarcity of this first edition (only 750 copies were printed), together with the obvious quality of the typography, binding and content, have made *The Shield Mares* much sought after by collectors, and the amount they have been willing to pay for a fine copy has risen almost astronomically.

It should be noted that the story has been reprinted in full as one of the chapters in *Some More Horse Tradin'*.

REVIEWS OF THE SHIELD MARES

With the two exceptions noted below, *The Shield Mares* received no immediate recognition from any media critics. Ben K. Green was an author unknown to the public and to the book reviewers, since *Horse Tradin',* published by Knopf a few weeks earlier, had not yet reached best-seller status, and the Encino Press, of Austin, Texas, was then known only to a relatively few Texas *aficionados* of fine printing. Moreover, according to William D. Wittliff, the founder and major domo of Encino, all 750 copies of *The Shield Mares* had been subscribed for in advance, and there simply weren't any copies available to send, gratis, to the press. Consequently, the first public mention of the book was the following brief notice:

Dallas Times-Herald, Sunday, October 15, 1967. A short paragraph by A. C. Greene (no kin to Ben K. Green) in the Sunday book page department "Writing & Reading This Week":

"Encino Press is publishing a limited edition of *The Shield Mares,* a short story by Ben K. Green, the author of *Horse Tradin'* (Knopf). The 750-copy edition, signed and in a slipcase, is designed by William Wittliff. A. C. Greene, *Times Herald* Book Editor, writes the introduction."

This notice does not do justice either to *The Shield Mares* or to A. C. Greene's introduction, from which the following is quoted:

"In general, I say meet as few authors as possible. Especially the ones whose work you like. Most of them are disappointing. You have read something into their books they never put there, or their characters of fiction are stronger and wiser than they are. Only now and then does a Ben K. Green come along to throw the old bone out to the dog. Ben not only lives up to the reader's picture of him. He surpasses it. He is exactly what his stories are. . . . A good imagination working with a real time, a real place, a real occasion, perceptively remembered, is a gift of rarity. It so seldom occurs that when it does we call it classic.

"In those terms, I would like to submit that Ben Green's *The Shield Mares* is a classic. 'Characterized by simple tailored lines in fashion year after year,' as one version of *Webster* puts it. . . . Green has established his place in letters in an immediate and (I predict) a lasting way. I am happy to know the man as well as the stories. And I relish both."

Shortly thereafter, *The Shield Mares* was reviewed at some length in *Southwestern Art, A Journal Devoted to Recognition of the Arts in the West and Southwest,* vol. II, no. 2, March, 1968, Austin, Texas. The review, signed "MBR" (for Mallory B. Randle, one of the periodical's editors), is well worth quoting from.

"Normally one doesn't review books which he has to buy or steal to read. It is a matter of pride. Either a publisher sends a review copy, or he doesn't get space.

"In the case of this excellent long-story by Ben K. Green, however, there had to be an exception. If you have made Green's acquaintance in *Horse Tradin'* . . . try to find a copy of *The Shield Mares.*

"'Cleanliness' is an attribute of which one rarely thinks when reading a book or story. . . . It is appropriate, however, to bring the word into consideration in this brief discussion of *Mares*. Not that there are discussions of fresh prairie winds, clear nights or good, clean earth. (It is not that kind of book. Green writes not *about* the land, but *from* it.)

"There is, however, a concentration in a book or story by Ben Green, a singleness of purpose, which renders [it] all-of-a-piece and full-to-the-brim. . . . One feels no lacks, nothing is missing. Each story provides a rather complete satisfaction. . . . Green deals only with horses and men, usually together, rarely (not at all in *Mares*) with a love story between man and woman. . . . And yet there is depth and variety, an awareness that the author, while telling of skill with horses, is somehow evoking a consciousness of the best human skills, sometimes even grace and nobility, all within the spare surroundings and using no other tools than those found within a horseman's life. . . .

"Even though the reader of Green's yarns finds himself in an old, almost forgotten Texas, reliving the activities of a little-known, outdated occupation, one feels that he is experiencing a sort of timeless microcosm.

"Green has, albeit unwittingly, answered the call which Walter Prescott Webb sounded some twenty years ago, when he wrote that southwestern artists and writers should look into and create from their own experience and environment — cultivate their own garden. Green's stories flow out of his southwestern experience just as natural and easy as the gait of a Shield Mare. The reader feels, when 'in the saddle,' that he could just keep on riding with a Shield Mare or any other Ben Green horse, as long and as often as Dr. Green gives him the chance."

Some six and one-half years after the above, *The Shield Mares* received a further appraisal (chiefly in bibliographical terms), in a book destined to be a landmark of scholarship, taste, and bookmaking in the Southwest, namely — *Printing Arts in Texas,* by Al Lowman. Roger Beachum, publisher. Austin, Texas, 1975. 107 pp., folio. Limited to 395 copies, of which 50 are a "de luxe" edition, specially signed and boxed. In discussing the contributions which William D. Wittliff has made to fine printing and its appreciation in Texas, the author, Al Lowman, says, on page 39:

"Wittliff has particular affection for *The Shield Mares,* his first collaboration with Ben K. Green, a splenetic veterinarian-turned-author whose raffish demeanor, suspenseful escapades, and rollicking prose style brand him as a Texas original. This book also appeared in 1967, only weeks after Knopf had introduced Green's writing to a nationwide audience with the publication of *Horse Tradin'*. The Encino Press title recounts Doc's adventures while trying to obtain a brood of fine-blooded mares from the old Shield Ranch along the middle Rio Grande border of southwest Texas.

"Fortunately his designers have never attempted to match Green's flamboyance in the format they have given his books. Which is not to say that Wittliff's approach to *The Shield Mares* is exactly decorous. The left half of the double title page identifies the author. His name appears in brown ink beneath a specially designed emblem depicting the letter 'G' in conjunction with a hypodermic syringe representing Doc's profession. On the facing page the title is printed in matching color beneath a stylized drawing of a shield. Throughout the book, then, the emblem is repeated in each left margin, balanced with the shield in the right margin. Green was so pleased with the device Wittliff had created for him that he adopted it as his personal totem and used it on stationery and on his subsequent books from Knopf and Northland Press.

"Wittliff's design of *The Shield Mares,* like Doc's telling of the story, wastes no effort settling to its purpose. Times Roman is not a typeface commonly used to make fine books, but here the designer has presented the best possible case for it, with straightforward typographical treatment on a fine Creme Blanc sheet. The binding is a buff-colored paper on boards that recalls vast reaches of border country turned sere and tawny under a relentless sun. . . . The final touch is a plainly fashioned slipcase with an unusually large title label."

¶ 9 *Horse Conformation as to Soundness and Performance.*

This work is the separately published collection of Green's articles on the structure and function of the horse which he published serially in the issues of *The Tally Book* from 1960 to 1962. In 1963 the articles were published together, in dif-

Ben K. Green

HORSE CONFORMATION

as to soundness and performance

A useful reference for the old horseman and a valuable guide for the amateur; written in easily understood terms

Horse Conformation—dust jacket, Northland Press edition

ferent format, as the first part of the book *Horse Conformation [and] Hoss Trades of Yesteryear.*

As a work by itself, however, *Horse Conformation as to Soundness and Performance* has been published in four versions: (A) A seventy-two-page pamphlet "first edition" of 1969, in white paper covers; (B) A seventy-four-page pamphlet "third edition" (actually the second) in 1972 in gray paper covers; (C) An eighty-page cloth bound version of 1975, in both a trade and (D) a limited edition. Each of these is described below; also (E) an advertising leaflet for (C) and (D).

(A) *Horse Conformation, first pamphlet edition.* The title and subtitle on the front cover read as follows:

HORSE
CONFORMATION
as to Soundness and Performance
A useful reference for the old horseman and a valuable guide for the amateur written in easily understood terms.

The title page, in its entirety, is worded:

HORSE
CONFORMATION
by Ben K. Green
Pioneer Stock Farm
Cumby, Texas
Copyright, 1969
All rights reserved, including the right
to reproduce this book or portions
thereof in any form.
First Edition

The book is bound in a white, stiff, semi-glossy paper, printed in bright blue and black. Within a heavy blue border on the front cover is a much reduced version of Tom Lea's horse diagram, Item 6, above. A one-eighth inch wide leftward extension of the blue border passes around the spine and serves to separate a half-tone picture of Ben Green from the Publisher's Note printed at the bottom of the back cover. Below the Publisher's Note is the statement that the book was "Written, published and distributed by Ben K. Green, P. O. Box 11, Greenville, Texas 75401."

From the bibliographer's standpoint the book is quite straightforward. The title page is page [1]. The reverse, numbered page 2, contains Green's "Foreword" in five paragraphs. Page 3 provides the Contents, listing the titles of the 17 chapters. Pages 4 through 72 contain the text and illustrations.

An error in the illustration on page 5 will serve to identify the true first edition. Three front views of a horse's head are placed side by side to illustrate the difference between excellent, good, and "worthless" head shapes. Unfortunately, the illustration for the worthless head appears over the caption for the "good" head, while the picture of the "good" head is captioned " 'Cute' little worthless head." Upon discovering the error, Green attempted to correct it by pen and black ink, using crossed arrows to transpose the captions, and reversing the numbers on illustrations 2 and 3 to conform to the references in the text. One wonders how many, if any, *uncorrected* copies got into circulation.

It should be noted that this separate edition of *Horse Conformation as to Soundness and Performance* contains an additional chapter (on pages 58 through 72) entitled "How to Tell the True Age of a Horse by the Teeth," which did not appear in the earlier book *Horse Conformation* [*and*] *Hoss Trades of Yesteryear,* and that the text of the present book is printed across the page, rather than in the double-column page format of the earlier book.

(B) *Horse Conformation, second pamphlet edition,* published in 1972. This edition differs from the first edition in the following respects:

First, Ben K. Green's name is listed as the author on the front cover, whereas it was omitted from the cover of the first edition.

Second, on the title page Green's address is changed to "Box 11, Greenville, Texas," rather than Cumby, Texas. The copyright date remains 1969. The words "Third Printing" appear below the copyright notice, although there was no edition or printing between this and the first edition. Green evidently considered *Horse Conformation and Hoss Trades of Yesteryear* as the true first printing, the "First edition" as the second printing, and this as the third.

Third, the covers of this second pamphlet are of light *gray* paper, printed in black and a lighter blue than on the first pamphlet. The back cover bears the picture of an older and much thinner Green, with a grizzled beard and chin whiskers, but the biographical sketch retains the original wording.

Fourth, two additional pages have been added. New page 73 is headed "Minimum Measurements Required of a Mare 14.2 Hands Tall, to qualify for Registration in the International Jockey Club Registry." More significantly, on new page 74 Green advertises his six books published up to that time, and notes a seventh, "A book on the color of horses, forthcoming (1973)." It was not actually published until 1974.

(C) *The revised hard back, trade edition.* Published by Northland Press, Flagstaff, Arizona, in August 1975, at $6.95.

Tall octavo (9¼ inches tall by 6¼ inches wide). 80 pp. Bound in brown binder's linen, with a square gold panel on the front cover as the background for a pacing horse in silhouette. The flat spine carries the title on one line, reading "Horse Conformation as to soundness and performance / Ben K.

Green." in gold. The endsheets are of a deep orange wove paper, the free endsheet being pasted to the half-title.

The book collates as follows: Page [i] half-title, which is pasted to the front free endsheet; [ii] blank; [iii] the title page, reading "Ben K. Green / [horizontal ornament] Horse / Conformation / as to soundness and / performance / Northland Press" / [publisher's device in light brown] / [iv] "Copyright 1969 by Ben K. Green / All Rights Reserved / First Printing of Revised Edition / August 1975 / ISBN 0–87358–135–0 / Library of Congress Catalog Card Number 74–82362 / Composed and Printed in the United States of America." Page v "Contents." [vi] blank; pages vii and viii "Preface." Pages numbered 1 through 80, the text.

The jacket is of white calendered paper printed in black and burnt orange. Its front flap states the price of $6.95, and contains a well-written and informative résumé of the book's contents, including the information that "Dr. Green finished the final revisions for this new edition just weeks before his death in 1974."

The back flap of the jacket contains the same gray-bearded picture of Green used on the back cover of the second pamphlet edition, but with a newly written biographical sketch listing his writings published by Northland Press, i.e., *The Color of Horses, A Thousand Miles of Mustangin', The Last Trail Drive Through Downtown Dallas,* and the four-volume set of *Ben Green Tales.*

For this edition the type has been completely reset, transforming what had been an economically produced pamphlet in paper covers into a handsomely printed and attractively bound volume. A similar transformation has been made in the illustrations, many of which have been redrawn by a professional artist (*anonymous*), with necessary re-numbering of the captions to accommodate to the references in the text. The new pictures add much to the book. There is also a new chapter, "Conformation of Brood Mares," beginning on page 65.

(D) *Revised hard back, limited edition,* 75 copies, signed by the publishers.

The covers of the limited edition are bound in rough-textured maroon buckram, with a black binder's linen spine on which the title is stamped in gold as on the trade edition. Endsheets are of the same orange paper used in the trade edition. There are short yellow and brown silk headbands at the top and foot of the spine, and the top edge of the pages is stained a dark brown.

Internally the limited edition is identical with the trade edition, except for the insertion at the front of a limitation page (on laid paper, rather than the wove paper of the text) reading as follows:

> Ben Green passed away October 5, 1974, on the road from South Dakota to Texas. He had finished his revisions for this new edition only a few weeks before. He had been in good spirits, and he died on the road, just as he had lived.
>
> This limited edition of 75 copies of *Horse Conformation* has been created as a tribute to Ben who always looked forward to limited editions of his books. It has been numbered and signed by the publisher and editor of Northland Press. This is number___.
>
> [Signatures] Paul Weaver Jim Howard

The de luxe edition is housed in a substantial slipcase, covered in the same closely woven black cloth used on the spine of the book. The silhouette of a pacing horse on a square gold background is stamped on the box to the right of the opening. The publisher's price for the limited edition, $75.00.

(E) Advertising leaflet, folded to make 4 pages, entitled "Horse Conformation As to Soundness and Performance. A Useful Reference for the Old Horseman and a Valuable Guide for the Amateur, Written in Easily Understood Terms."

Printed in black and blue on shiny paper, reproducing the covers of the first *Horse Conformation* pamphlet. The center spread contains a reduced printing of the large chart "How to Tell the True Age of a Horse by the Teeth." There is also an announcement that the hardback book *Horse Conformation* [*and*] *Hoss Trades of Yesteryear* "is now out of print and is quoted on rare book lists at $25.00 per copy and more. Written, published and distributed by Ben K. Green, P. O. Box 11, Greenville, Texas."

REVIEWS OF HORSE CONFORMATION IN THE REVISED HARD BACK EDITION

Weekly Livestock Reporter, Fort Worth, April 22, 1976. Review by Ted Gouldy under the heading "Worthwhile Books." Excerpt: "Knowledgeable horse owners often make mistakes, and many of these mistakes can be avoided by the simple application of diagnosis of the structural pro's and con's described in this book. . . . Anyone interested in horses, training horses and using horses, will find this book a treasure trove of information. . . ."

Books of the Southwest, A Critical Checklist of Current Americana. Compiled Monthly by Donald M. Powell, University of Arizona Library, Tucson, and Betty Rosenberg, University of California, Los Angeles. Number 204, October, 1975. Brief notice, unsigned, reading in full: "This is the last word from the late Ben Green who has long amused us with such splendid books as *Horse Tradin'* and *Wild Cow Tales.* This, of course, is strictly for the horseman, but there are many of those in our Southwest."

Sioux Falls [S.D.] *Argus-Leader.* October 19, 1975. Untitled review, signed "D.H.S." Excerpt: "A veterinarian recognized as one of the world's great horse experts wrote this book 'to emphasize and illustrate the horse as an animal of living, mechanical perfection.' Attention is centered upon stride, ability to carry weight, the conformation of brood mares and how to tell a horse's true age by his teeth, along with problems often little understood even by well-informed horsemen. The simple concise text is accompanied by clearly drawn diagrams."

The Western Horseman. February, 1976. Unsigned review, not titled. Excerpts:

"This is a revised edition of a book first published in 1969. And it adds still more credit to the memory of the author, who passed away in 1974. Far from being dry and boring, the book is a real eye-opener, and will add much to the horse know-how of almost any reader. . . .

"Especially enlightening is the chapter on vision. . . . Through the explanation of how and what a horse sees, the reader will understand why a horse may suddenly shy at something that has been in plain sight, and why a horse that constantly flicks one ear is likely to have vision problems in the eye on that same side of his head.

"There's much more to learn from this book, including why you should never clip the whiskers around your horse's nostrils and muzzle. The one section that may be controversial is the section dealing with forward-seat riding—Ben Green didn't think much of it and gives the reasons why. . . ."

El Paso Herald-Post, Saturday, December 27, 1975. Untitled review by Nancy Hamilton. Excerpts:

"Dr. Green finished this revision of his 1969 book just weeks before his death in 1974. . . . He wrote the first book on how color occurs on horses, as well as fiction [?] about ranch life and has a knack for good story-telling. . . . Even though this little book has to do with the technical aspects of how horses are formed and function, the material is interesting and thorough. The illustrations are as direct and clear as the writing. . . ."

El Paso Times, Sunday, September 28, 1975. Unsigned review under the heading "Book Briefs; New and Recommended." Excerpt:

"Dr. Green considers the various parts of the horse's anatomy and the ways in which these function and interrelate to affect the animal's soundness and performance."

¶ 10 Der betrogene Rosstäuscher. Zwölf authentische Geschichten aus dem Wilden Westen. Von Ben K. Green. Nymphenberger Verlagshandlung. [Title page, which translated, reads "The Out-traded Horse Trader. Twelve authentic stories from the Wild West, by Ben K. Green. Nymphenburg Publishers."] [Munich, Germany, 1969.]

The copyright page, the verso of the title page, reads: "Aus dem Amerikanischen von Alexander Bergengruen [i.e., "translated from 'American-English' by Alexander Bergengruen.] Titel-nr. 0704."

"Die Geschichten dieses Buches sind dem 1967 im Verlag Alfred A. Knopf, Inc., New York, erschienenen Band "Horse Tradin' " © 1963, 1965, 1967 by Ben K. Green, entnommen." [The stories in this book were published in 1967 by Alfred A. Knopf, Inc., New York, under the title "Horse Tradin'," etc.]

"Nymphenburger Verlagshandlung GmbH., München. Alle Rechte, auch der fotomechanischen Vervielfältigung / und des auszugsweisen Absdrucks, vorbehalten / Satz und Druck: F. Puster, Graphischer Groosbetrieb, Regensburg. Printed in Germany."

The book is 5 by 8 inches in size, has 258 pages plus one page of ads for other books by the publisher, and is nicely bound in blue cloth with a white paper label, printed in black, at the top of the spine. The top edge is stained a bright red.

The dust jacket is of white calendered paper, with a modernistic drawing of a bucking horse and the head and shoulders of a fat-faced man in a big hat, in four colors.

The twelve stories in the book, selected from the twenty in *Horse Tradin',* are entitled "Das Pferd, das stets zusammenbrach," ("Gypsy Hoss Trade" in *Horse Tradin'*); "Ein phantastischer Hengst, dieser Rebel Commander," ("Rebel Commander"); "Die Frau mit dem Fohlen" ("Nubbin' "); "Ein Pony als Medizin," ("Angel"); "Ein schläfriger Teufel," ("Maniac Mule"); "Immer im Kreis herum," ("Matched Mares"); "Der betrogene Rosstäuscher," used as the title for the book, and meaning, as indicated above, "The Out-traded Horse Trader," or "The Smart Horse Trader Out-Smarted."

In *Horse Tradin'* the story is "Easter Lily." The next chapter is entitled "Pferde kontra Pferdestärken," ("When Big Horses Went Out of Style — Almost"); "Ein fast tadelloses Tier" ("Traveling Mare"); "Traue nicht mal dem Herrn Pfarrer" ("The Parson's Mare, Bessie"); "Wie man Esel jung färbt" ("The Gray Mules"); and finally "Indianer können mehr als reiten" ("The Schoolmarm and Ol' Nothin' "). These German titles are not, of course, literal translations of the original English versions, but they (hopefully) provide for the German reader an approximation of the meaning of the originals.

Perhaps the problem of translating the *flavor* of the original is insoluble, and it must be admitted that the flavor of Green's writings is a good part of their captivating charm. The transmitting of the flavor of the original writing into another language is the great challenge to any translator; how well this flavor has been transmitted in *Der betrogene Rosstäuscher* can be known only to those fortunate enough to command a knowledge of both colloquial German and colloquial Texan-American.

But regardless of where he lives, the American reader familiar with the books of our western states can well imagine the problems faced by any "outlander" who has to translate into a foreign language such Americanisms as barbecue, schoolmarm, shack, Model T, swap, creek (not the Indian tribe, by the way), "set a spell," kids, and spooky. And what does he do with such Texanisms as a bowl of chili, Crazy Water, pinto, a batch of grub, and norther?

After all, we North Americans have enjoyed the beauties of Schiller and Goethe, the good-hearted satire of Cervantes's *Don Quixote,* the romantic adventures of D'Artagnan and his Three Musketeers (not to mention the pre-science fiction of Jules Verne), and the glories and tragedy of Rome in *Quo Vadis,* all translated into our language from their German,

Der betrogene Rosstäuscher—dust jacket and title page

Spanish, French, and Polish originals, to mention only a few. We can only hope that those across the water who enjoy reading books about "The Great American West" can get as much pleasure from these as we have from theirs.

Early in 1976 I wrote the publisher ordering additional copies, and received a reply, in English, to the effect that the book was no longer in stock, i.e., out of print, in Germany.

¶ 11 *Wild Cow Tales*. Published in (A) The trade edition in cloth; (B) A limited edition, signed and boxed; (C) A paperback edition. These are described below.

(A) *Wild Cow Tales,* hardbound edition. By Ben K. Green, Alfred A. Knopf, New York, 1969. Illustrated by Lorence Bjorklund. [On copyright page]: "This is a Borzoi Book published by Alfred A. Knopf, Inc. First Edition. Copyright 1969 by Ben K. Green. All rights reserved, etc."

Octavo, 12 preliminary pages, 306 text pages. The first "trade," i.e. regular, edition is bound in brown binder's linen, with the title stamped vertically in gold along the spine, and with a western style hat stamped in gold on the front cover. The back cover is bare except for the publisher's Borzoi dog symbol blind stamped at the lower right.

"A Note About the Author" appears on page [307], while "A Note on the Type," crediting the typographic and binding design to Bonnie Spiegel of the publisher's staff, occupies page [308].

The dust jacket of the first edition is printed in black, red, and brown on cream paper, and bears the date "3/69" on the lower left corner of the rear flap. A full-page photograph of a benign Doc Green, in white hat, working jacket, and unshaven phiz, occupies the entire back of the dust jacket.

(B) *Wild Cow Tales,* limited edition, signed Ben K.

Wild Cow Tales—dust jacket

Green. The book is bound in light tan buckram, with the title stamped in gold on a black leather label on the spine. There is a dust jacket of transparent acetate, and the volume is boxed in a grey cardboard slipcase. According to the limitation page the book is limited to 300 copies. But I and others have seen copies numbered as high as 320 and more! When I asked Doc Green "How come?" he said that he had received a stack of limitation sheets from the publisher, and "I just signed and numbered them all without bothering to count." In a checklist of books illustrated by Lorence Bjorklund, Jeff C. Dykes, compiler of the monumental *Fifty Great Western Illustrators, a Bibliographical Checklist* (Northland Press, 1975), explains the discrepancy by stating that a late change in the printing order raised the number to 350 copies, but the book was issued without changing the number printed on the limitation page.

Collectors of the limited edition of *Wild Cow Tales* should be aware of an unfortunate defect which has developed in the binding. In all copies I have examined, the thick transparent acetate jacket has stuck more or less firmly to the surface of the black title label on the spine, and efforts to remove the jacket from the book have caused some of the gold stamping to come off with it, along with portions of the polished surface of the label. After some experimentation I found that I could remove the jacket without damage to gold or the label by squirting gasoline-type lighter fluid into the sticking areas and carefully peeling the jacket from the spine.

Collectors should also note the presence of a variant slipcase. Green was, according to Mrs. Rosemary Barker, not satisfied with the original gray paper-covered box provided by the publisher, Knopf, and had about ten more substantial slipcases made for his copies by a bookbinder. These were covered in a cream-colored laid paper more nearly matching the color of the buckram of the limited edition casings. For sticklers to detail, the sides of the publisher's box measure 1/16th of an inch thick, and the head and foot 3/16ths, while those of Green's box measure approximately twice as thick.

(C) *Wild Cow Tales,* the paperback edition. Ballantine Books, New York. [On copyright page]: "Copyright 1969 by Ben K. Green. This edition published by arrangement with Alfred A. Knopf, Inc. First printing: February, 1974." The book is 4 by 7 inches in size, and is a page for page facsimile of the hardback edition, photographically reduced to smaller size. The covers are of black stiff paper. The front cover bears a 3- by 4-inch painting in color signed "McCarthy," showing a mounted cowboy leading a pack horse; this is somewhat surprising, since all the other illustrations in the paperback are by Bjorklund, as in the hardback edition.

In *Wild Cow Tales* Green demonstrates an encyclopedic and very practical knowledge of cow psychology, which he puts to good use in a number of difficult situations. He is called on as an expert to round up wild cattle escaped from the stock car of a wrecked train near Bowie, Texas; a Kansas City bank hires him to corral and deliver Scotch Highland cattle scattered on a mountain ranch in the Colorado Rockies, in the face of a tough old Scotsman who had mortgaged the cattle to the bank; he buys eight wild and wily longhorn steers running loose in the mesquite brush, and they defy all his efforts to catch them except the last one. Not the least interesting is the picture Green gives of the inner working and colorful personalities of the vanished Fort Worth Stockyards in their heyday, when "Fo't Wuth" was the cowboy's Mecca for fun and hell-raisin', and the ranch-owner's market and banking center.

The book did not achieve the widespread national popularity of *Horse Tradin',* perhaps because there are more people interested in reading about horses than about wild cows. Nevertheless, it was popular enough to convince Knopf that a paperback edition would be profitable, as it has undoubtedly been. More importantly, the book won for Green the following citation from the prestigious Southwestern Library Association.

(D) *Award from the Southwestern Library Association.* 1970. Broadside in two sizes, designed by William D. Wittliff, The Encino Press, Austin, Texas. It reads:

> In recognition of a work which through its colorful & distinguished writing, its keen wit & its vivid portrayal of a vanishing part of the cattle industry, makes a unique & lasting contribution to the literature of the region, this citation is awarded to Ben K. Green for his book, *Wild Cow Tales.* The Southwestern Library Association, 23rd Biennial Conference, Fort Worth, 1970.

The presentation broadside measures 15½ by 11½ inches in size, and is printed around the four sides of a rectangle.

Green also had Wittliff print up 1,000 smaller copies, reduced in size to 8½ by 11 inches, which Green could insert in copies of his book. See Lutz, Willis J. *William D. Wittliff, A Bibliography,* item C 23, Dallas, 1975.

WILD COW TALES BOOK REVIEWS

Lexington Leader, Lexington, Kentucky. Wednesday, March 26, 1969. Book review in the column entitled "Leanin' On The Rail," by Frank T. Phelps. The reviewer says, in part:

"Most of these yarns happened in the late 1920s and early 1930s, when cattle were cheap and wild cattle were worth about half as much as cattle that could be handled horseback. . . . So he took range delivery of the outlaw cattle that had evaded roundups and learned to hide in dense brush, river bottoms or mountains. Not only were such cattle hard to catch and harder to drive to a railhead when they were caught, but they were likely to be murderously mean as well. Dr. Green . . . has a sharp wit and a shrewd mind; and he was rarely outsmarted in any trade, although that was not because others did not try.

"He is a rarity, a genuine cowboy with intelligence and understanding enough to describe the economic and social changes that have affected the horse and cattle business in the Far Southwest. His explanation of [these changes] is clearer than a sociologist or economist would probably make it. . . . But Dr. Green lets nothing stand in the way of a good yarn, and he has a rare flair for spinning an intriguing story. *Wild Cow Tales* will make a treasured companion volume to *Horse Tradin'* among those who relish authentic accounts of the real West in place of the usual hoked-up pap we get on television and in the movies."

Fort Worth Star-Telegram, Sunday, March 16, 1969. Review entitled "Yarn-Spinner Spins More," by Leonard Sanders. He writes:

"The author . . . probably is not as old as he implies in conversation (which is about two years older than Moses), but he was a horse trader and cattle buyer in the late 1920s and 1930s when Fort Worth was the hub for a major portion of the cattle industry, and his yarns are as obviously authentic as smoke from a mesquite camp fire. This authenticity was apparent to the editors at Knopf a couple of years ago when they received some of the stories Green had put down on paper. They were put into a book, *Horse Tradin',* and the result was one of those rarities that renew faith in U.S. publishing and readership. Reviews were enthusiastic, the sale reports were excellent, and the book is now being proclaimed 'a minor classic.'

"Green's second collection of stories, *Wild Cow Tales,* was released last week, and the editors at Knopf have said privately that these thirteen stories are even better than those in *Horse Tradin'*. The point is debatable, but immaterial. They are equally good, but of different flavor, so any comparison is personal. . . . The stories are replete with broken bones (Green's) and scraped hide (Green's, horses' and steers'). He reveals his tricks of the trade. Some might not be approved by the SPCA, but then, there never was a Society for the Prevention of Cruelty to Cowboys. . . .

"Green, who in these two books has demonstrated his ability to rope and tie editors and readers, is busy now pulling books out of the brush. He has just been offered a two-book contract on the basis of the success of *Horse Tradin'* and advance reports on *Wild Cow Tales.*"

The Dallas Times-Herald, Dallas, Texas, April 6, 1969. Review entitled "Ol' Ben's Hickese Is a Joy to Read," by P. R. [Paul Richard] Bosse, a Dallas bookseller. [Mr. Bosse is the able proprietor of the Aldredge Book Store, and a fellow member of the Antiquarian Booksellers Association of America.] He says, *inter alia,* "Green is perhaps the most gifted of all Texas story tellers . . . possibly because he first dictates his material into a tape recorder. Dialect writing is, praise Calliope, today seldom encountered, but Green writes in a sort of sophisticated hickese. It is a most difficult medium and usually comes out either hokey, offensive, or precocious, but Green masters the form with a unique artistry. *Wild Cow Tales* is an entertaining collection of anecdotes of the author outwitting cows, ranchers, and bankers. Since there is less imaginative larceny in cow people than in horse traders, this book will disappoint some readers of the author's previous efforts, but the quality of writing and material remains at the same high level. . . . It is a pretty safe bet that a century hence readers will still delight in his writings."

The Weekly Livestock Reporter, Fort Worth, Texas, Thursday, March 20, 1969. Review entitled "No Instant History These," in "Stuph & Thangs" column, no author shown. The reviewer, writing in country dialect, says in part: "We been personally acquainted with Doc [Green] fer a number of years and we git along fairly well despite the fack that our conversations are reputedly audible for several blocks. . . . Doc is a little guy with the tenacity of a cuckle burr and the outgin' personality of a prickly pear, however, the day is usually brighter after we clash.

"Fokes who read *Horse Tradin'* will no doubt lay down some rubber gittin' down to buy Doc's *Wild Cow Tales* to add to their collection. These books are actually a kind of History that gives insight into the Cow Country that is new to most of the populace. . . . After readin' Doc's Documentaries you will understand more about the people who opened up the West and have kept it fairly open since."

The El Paso Times, El Paso, Texas, March 30, 1969. Review entitled "Wild Cow Tales," by Leon C. Metz, one column. Excerpts:

"Most of us think of cows as docile animals that give milk, or as steers that stare in a blank, unthreatening, cud-chewing manner when we drive too close. Green, however, expresses interest only in the wild ones that spend their lives in the brush, avoiding roundups, and are meaner than a rattlesnake with a hot match under its belly. . . . Wild cattle will gore you, trample you, and frequently outsmart you. . . . Thus the call goes out for a specialist, one who thinks like these critters and who will risk rope burns and brush scratches to bring them to market. It is an interesting life, and anyone who participates will always have his saddlebags chuck full of tales to spin.

"Green, of course, is a natural for all this. . . . The stories are entirely colloquial, full of tradin', and sellin', and blowin' and chewin'. Some are pure corn. Yet the book has an honest, sincere appeal, something which will make an entire family feel a little closer and a little warmer and a little happier after reading it."

From an unknown source, a review entitled "For Those Who've Wondered Why Cowboys Love Horses, and Hate Cows," by "D.W." The review reads, in part:

"Author Ben K. Green is a gnarled old cattleman whose eyes are squinty from too much sun, face leathery from too much of the same. The reader doesn't have to see a picture of the man . . . it's clearer than a photograph as the reader lines his eyes across pages that turn into miles of Texas prairie and mesquite country, and is alternately frozen in winter, scorched in the summer, torn by thorn thickets, and attacked and outsmarted by the most stupid and ornery of all God's creatures — the Texas range cow.

"There is much genuine range humor in these pages — humor that is neither raucous nor subtle, humor that may perhaps even be lost on the reader who has never uttered a heartfelt curse at a cow brute that has eluded him, stepped on him, knocked him down and generally given him a much better perspective of his insignificant place in the universe.

"But there is more than humor. Ben Green has put down on paper a piece of life, a life-style if you will, that once existed but is no more. . . . There is in this book the answer to why wealthy men support herds of cattle, and why poor men will support as many as they can — and you'd better believe it goes far beyond tax writeoffs and other such mundane things.

"Many people who read *Wild Cow Tales* will not really understand. They will think they have read only a collection of stories . . . about a young nearly always broke cowpuncher who turned a profit buying range-delivered cattle, rounding them up, and shipping them off to the Fort Worth stockyards.

"But for those who do understand, there will be a tear or a smile, and many pleasant memories."

¶ 12 *Ben K. Green Back to Back. Texas Cow Horses & the Vermont Maid; Mr. Undertaker & the Cleveland Bay Horse.* 1970: The Encino Press: Austin.

Oblong 12mo, 6¼ inches tall by 9¼ inches long. 51 pp plus unnumbered last page colophon. Bound in cherry red boards with a buff paper label, 4½ by 3½ inches, on the front cover, depicting a smiling, youthful Ben K. Green in working jacket and white hat, with his hands in his pants pockets, one of his few three-quarter length pictures. The flat spine bears the title in black ink "Ben K. Green Back to Back." The end-sheets are of the same red paper used on the covers, and the book is signed in black ink, "Ben K. Green," on the first blank preliminary page.

The ending colophon reads, in part: "This book has been issued in an edition of 850 signed copies of which this is copy number ____. Design by William D. Wittliff."

The printing is in black ink on buff paper throughout, with the text occupying only the inner half of each page. The outer half of the page contains the running title, printed in red in large capitals, with the folio, or page number, in red at the bottom.

The effect is both unusual and handsome, although the type used in printing the text is, to my taste, several points too small, and tends to be overpowered by the bold red running heads.

The book is boxed in a lightweight cardboard slipcase of

BEN K. GREEN

TEXAS
COW HORSES
& THE VERMONT
MAID

MR.
UNDERTAKER &
THE CLEVELAND
BAY HORSE

BACK TO BACK

1970 : THE ENCINO PRESS : AUSTIN

Ben K. Green Back to Back—title page

the same color as the book, with a 4 by 6-inch buff paper label containing a slightly reduced version of the title page.

The two stories, "Texas Cow Horses and the Vermont Maid," and "Mr. Undertaker and the Cleveland Bay Horse," were published here for the first time. They were later reprinted as chapters in *Some More Horse Tradin'*.

Although published three years later than *The Shield Mares* (1967), and in an edition of 100 more copies (850 as compared to 750), the book has been long out of print, and is now almost as hard to find as its predecessor, although not yet bringing so high a price. Aside from its intrinsic desirability as a handsome vehicle for two good stories, it is wanted both by Wittliff collectors and Ben K. Green *aficionados*. The combination of the two demands will undoubtedly result in a constant increase in the price.

¶ 13 *Living Texas, a Gathering of Experiences*. Compiled and Edited by A. C. Greene. Jointly published by Hendrick-Long Company [Dallas] and The Encino Press [Austin] 1970. Illustrated with woodcuts by Barbara Whitehead.

Octavo, 8¾ inches tall by 6¾ inches wide. 209pp, white pictorial cloth. Design by William D. Wittliff.

This is a supplemental reader for eighth grade classes in social studies and Texas history. It contains two Green stories, "Homer's Last Mule," from *Horse Tradin'*, on page 109, and "The One that Got Away," from *Wild Cow Tales*, page 114.

According to Lutz, *William D. Wittliff, A Bibliography*, item A 38 (1975), *Living Texas* was published in two editions, a "demonstration edition" of 300 copies to be used in soliciting orders from secondary schools, and a regular edition for actual school use, with only minor differences between the two. Green's stories contain two illustrations by Whitehead.

Green stories in *Living Texas*

¶ 14 "Mr. Undertaker and the Cleveland Bay Horse." The second story in *Ben K. Green Back to Back,* above, reprinted in *Persimmon Hill,* vol. 1, no. 3, for Winter, 1971, beginning on page 14. *Persimmon Hill, A Quarterly of the West,* is a publication of the National Cowboy Hall of Fame and Western Heritage Center at Oklahoma City, Oklahoma, with Dean Krakel as Managing Editor and Don Hedgpeth as [then] Editor. The story is accompanied, on page 19, by a full-page account of Green and his work written by Don Hedgpeth, surmounted by a three-quarter-length photograph of a smiling, unshaven Ben Green in his working clothes.

¶ 15 *The Village Horse Doctor: West of the Pecos.* Published in (A) a trade edition in cloth; (B) a signed limited edition, boxed; and (C) a paperback edition. Each of these is described below.

(A) *The Village Horse Doctor: West of the Pecos,* hardbound trade edition. Ben K. Green. Alfred A. Knopf, New York 1971. Illustrated by Lorence Bjorklund.

306pp, plus "A Note About the Author" on p [309] and "A Note on the Type" on p [310].

"First Edition" under copyright notice on verso of title page.

The first printing of the regular edition is bound in very light tan binder's linen, with a horse's head stamped in copper gilt on the front cover, and the title vertically in copper on the spine. The top edge is stained a burgundy color.

The collation, again, is unusual for a commercially published book. The free endpaper is blank on both sides. The recto of the first prelim [i] is blank, while its verso [ii] carries the advertisement, "Also by Ben K. Green / *Horse Tradin'* / *Wild Cow Tales* / These are Borzoi Books / Published in

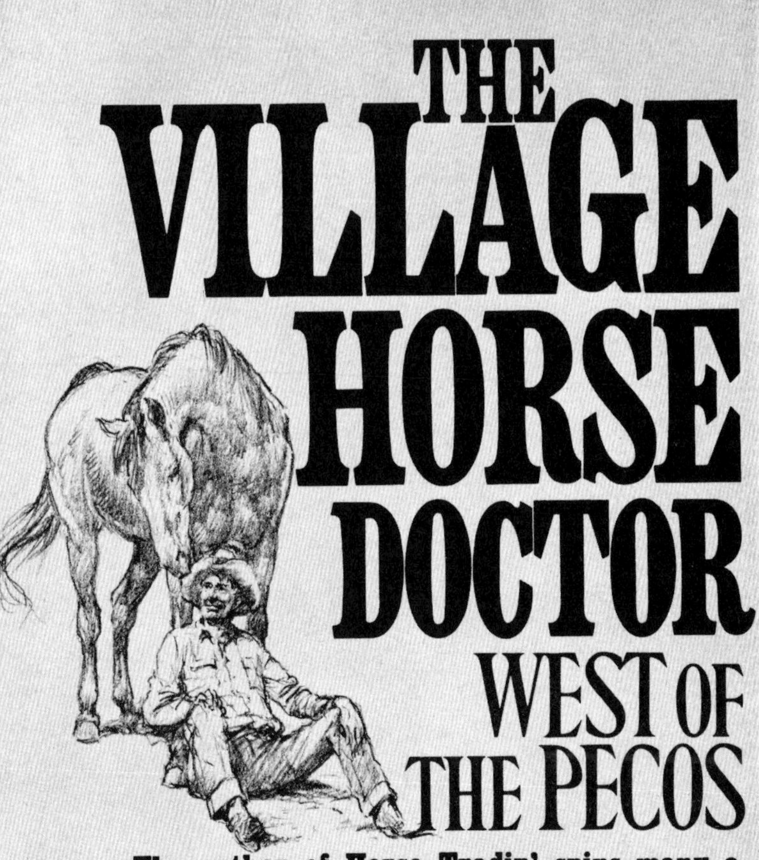

The Village Horse Doctor—dust jacket

New York by / Alfred A. Knopf." The recto of the following page [iii] bears the half title, reading *The Village / Horse Doctor: / West of the Pecos.* On its verso [iv] is a fine charcoal pencil drawing, untitled, of a rock tor of New Mexico or Arizona by Bjorklund. The recto [v] is the title page, which reads: "Ben K. Green / The Village / Horse Doctor: / West of the Pecos / [Borzoi dog] / Alfred A. Knopf New York 1971 / Illustrated by Lorence Bjorklund." The copyright page [vi] provides the usual information, followed by the words "First Edition." (Subsequent issues are indicated by "Second," "Third," etc. "Printing." Page [vii] contains Green's four-paragraph introduction, quoted below. The verso [viii] is blank. Pages [ix] and [x] hold the table of contents, while [xi], actually page 1 of the text, though not numbered, repeats the half-title, for some reason known only to the book's designer. The verso [p. 2] of the half-title contains a well-executed shaded map of far West Texas and New Mexico depicting the range of Doc Green's veterinary practice. The following page [3] provides the title for the first chapter, entitled "Smart? Horse Doctor." Pages [4] and [5] have a double-page spread of a pencil drawing by Bjorklund, with the first paragraph of the text in the upper left corner. The text continues on page 6, the first page to bear a folio.

The dust jacket of the first edition is worthy of some attention. It is printed in brown, black, and maroon inks on cream wove paper, but with the front and back flaps in off-white to match the text paper. The front flap shows the price of the book as $6.95, with the figures slightly askew. The back flap bears the date 4/71 at the bottom right, and a credit "Photo: Narramore" vertically along the fold-over, referring to the full-page picture of Ben Green which occupies the entire back of the dust jacket. The jacket was designed by Charles Schmalz, and includes a drawing by Bjorklund.

(B) *The Village Horse Doctor: West of the Pecos,* limited edition. The book is limited to 250 copies, numbered and signed "Ben K. Green." The limitation page is pasted in following the front free endsheet, and reads:

> Of the first edition of THE VILLAGE HORSE DOCTOR *West of the Pecos* two hundred and fifty copies have been printed on special paper and specially bound. Each copy is signed by the author and numbered. No.____.

The covers are bound in a light tan natural buckram, with Green's "syringe-G" design stamped in gold in the center of the front cover. The spine is in light brown buckram, heavily gilt, and the book is covered with a transparent acetate jacket. The cardboard box is covered in mustard-colored paper, and decorated with Bjorklund drawings printed in brown. The original price of the limited edition: $20.00.

(C) *The Village Horse Doctor: West of the Pecos,* paperback edition. Ben K. Green. Illustrated by Lorence Bjorklund. Ballantine Books, New York. [On copyright page]: "This edition published by arrangement with Alfred A. Knopf, Inc. First Printing; August, 1974. Cover art by Bozzo. . . . Ballantine Books, a Division of Random House, Inc." 12MO, 4⅜ by 7¼ inches, bound in stiff plastic-coated yellow paper and printed in green, black, and brown, with a white spine. 306 pp. A reduced facsimile of the text of the regular edition, with the redundant preliminary pages omitted, and three pages of ads for Ballantine Books inserted at the back.

Because Green's short preface sheds some light on that portion of his life spent in far West Texas (a portion not entirely devoid of unfriendly controversy, the causes of which must await the work of a biographer) I reproduce it here in full.

> Howdy. *The Village Horse Doctor* is an accurate account of my true experiences during my years of practice in the Far

> Southwest as the first veterinary doctor at Fort Stockton, Texas.
>
> I offer no apologies for having written the true facts about the conditions in this desert country, and I have the highest regard for a rugged breed of people who were ever grateful for my efforts and so charitable of my many mistakes.
>
> My life has been rough but it has never been dull, and the time covered by these chapters is probably the roughest and the furtherest from being dull as any years that I have so far spent on this earth.
>
> You will find no bibliographies or other list of references in this book since all the material is that of the Village Horse Doctor himself. Ben K. Green.

The book closes with an unusual essay by Green entitled "The Desert," in which he displays again the admixture of romanticism and practicality which permeates his tales. Here is a portion:

> Those of the human race who are natives of the desert and don't know any better expect less from it and suffer less from disappointments. Those who have migrated to the desert and have become trapped by its mystery and the splendors of its sunrises, and the fascinating beauty of the desert sunsets, oftimes convince themselves that the desert offers great promise. . . . But the man who intends to earn a living from the surfaces of the desert should bring himself to realize that the desert has never promised man nor animal anything but isolation and solitude, and all the rest of the brainstorms that the human race may have nurtured about *promise* should be evaluated rather in the light of challange than promise; the desert challenges man every morning when the blistering sun moves beyond that early morning grandeur. After ten years of drouth the ingenuity of man made a very small shadow under the scorching sun. . . .

REVIEWS OF VILLAGE HORSE DOCTOR

Denver Post, August 29, 1971. Review entitled "Doc Green Tells Homey Tales," by Red Fenwick in his column "Ridin' the Range." "Human, warm and homey, Doc's book is like a summer rain in the middle of a long drought. It's refreshing by the very absence of sex and social complications so dominant in today's so-called literature.

"In endorsing the book for all members of the family I mustn't overlook the illustrations beautifully and understandingly done by the artist, Lorence Bjorklund.

"Doc writes knowingly about mama cows and people mamas, big animals and little animals, among them a family of skunks, and ranch folks and Mexican sheepherders.

"Doc has treated horses, cattle, sheep and other animals including a few human beings, all the way from the Pecos to the Gila and the upper Rio Grande. And I'd say Doc Green knows more about horses than most horses know."

Lubbock (Texas) *Avalanche-Journal,* Friday, November 5, 1971. Review entitled "Autographs New Book; Author Comes to 'Party,'" written by Tanner Laine of the *Avalanche-Journal* staff. Excerpts:

"Dr. Ben K. Green of Cumby, Texas, author of the book *The Village Horse Doctor,* came to Lubbock Thursday with a pretty good prescription for both owners and their animals; 'Take a big dose of common sense and be natural—be what you are without putting on.'

"'Doc' Green tells you himself that he had little formal schooling. What he doesn't tell you but what you catch quickly is, he has a perfect (though sometimes profane) corral-side manner and plenty of natural wit.

"The good 'doctor' was the first to hang up a shingle out in the trans-Pecos country. And he didn't start small. His rounds of practice were 420 miles north-south and 360 miles east-west. He covered them by all means known to man—shank's mare, horseback, buckboard, and his old standby for long hauls, a beat-up old coupe on whose body panels he kept his books in chalk.

"His writings, although he stoutly denies being a writer, instead declaring 'I'm just an author; somebody else writes it down,' are a nostalgic and hilarious journey into a spacious yesterday, refreshing in this hurried day. His is a canny mix of science and 'horse sense.'"

Fort Worth Star Telegram, May 9, 1971. Review entitled "Green Spins More Yarns," by Leonard Sanders. He says, in part:

"Most yarn-spinners eventually either run out of tales, grow repetitious, or else enter a slow decline as their font of experience is expended. But Ben K. Green, the Cumby cowboy, veterinarian, horse trader and general all-around character, just seems to pick up steam as he goes along.

"*The Village Horse Doctor* is Green's best book to date. Always readable, Green has settled into a relaxed style that allows the intrinsic humor in his stories to surface with more ease. The yarns are assembled into a sort of loose plot. In the opening chapter, Green describes his arrival in Fort Stockton in early 1944. En route to Mexico, he allowed himself to be talked into setting up shop as Fort Stockton's first practitioner of veterinary medicine. He and the town soon had reason to wonder if they both had made a mistake."

Publisher's Weekly, March 1, 1971. Brief unsigned review, containing the following comment on Green's writing style:

"Green's reminiscences are written in a simple loping cadence and are full of authentic imagery. He moves easily from chuckles to drama, telling of the people who became part of his life, his medical research, and the thousands of miles he traveled to treat sick livestock that nobody else could save."

¶ 16 *The Last Trail Drive Through Downtown Dallas.* Published in (A) hardbound trade edition; (B) limited edition; and (C) talking book edition.

(A) *The Last Trail Drive Through Downtown Dallas,* hardbound trade edition. Ben K. Green. Illustrated by Joe Beeler / Published by Northland Press / Flagstaff, Arizona.

The verso of the title page states: "Copyright 1971 / by / Ben K. Green / This edition limited to 1,750 copies / Library of Congress Catalog Number 75–150687 / SBN 87358–068–0." The colophon on the verso of page 73 states, "This book was set in the Aldus type of Herman Zapf and printed on Beckett Laid Text — Binding by Roswell."

Oblong 8vo, 9¼ inches wide by 8⅞ inches tall. 73 numbered pages, plus the un-numbered colophon page. The

The Last Trail Drive Through Downtown Dallas—
Joe Beeler illustration on page 5

binding of this edition is unusual: the spine is covered in bright red binder's linen, while the covers are in brown buckram.

The orange-red dust jacket is printed on a basic cream-colored stock, with front and rear inner flaps showing the cream and carrying brief biographies of the author and illustrator. The rear flap states definitely that "Ben K. Green is a doctor of veterinary medicine," and is "one of the world's greatest horse experts." The front of the jacket has a subtitle reading, "The True and Humorous Account of the Author's Early Venture into Big-Time Horse Trading." Price $8.50.

(B) *The Last Trail Drive Through Downtown Dallas,* limited edition. A special edition, limited to 100 copies, bound in one-half brown calf, with brown buckram cloth covers, boxed in a substantial slipcase. Each volume was numbered and signed by Green at the front on a special limitation page which bears an original pen and ink and wash drawing of a western scene (for example, a mounted cowboy lighting a cigarette; a western saddle; a trail herd look-out) by Joe Beeler. Although Joe Beeler's original drawings and paintings bring substantial prices, many collectors balked at paying the original $150.00 retail price for this limited edition, in which Beeler's original drawings varied rather widely in quality and detail.

Green himself was especially pleased with the picture on page 5 of the text showing him sitting under a tree and chewing on a straw, although Dallasites could question Beeler's verisimiltude in picturing the old Houston Street viaduct, which connects Dallas to Oak Cliff, as being arched over the railroad tracks leading into the Union Station (page 34). And older residents of Rockwall might have difficulty in recognizing Beeler's depiction of the entrance gate to their old City Park (following page 44).

The title of the book gives the impression that it concerns Dallas only, but this is far from the fact. Green's journey with his remuda involved trading and trailing adventures in a number of other North Texas towns, notably Marshall in Harrison County, northeast Texas, where he inveigles a bunch of Mexican railroad workers into putting on an impromptu Sunday rodeo with the promise of a barbecued *cabrito* (goat) dinner and one dollar for each unbroke horse they could tame.

The publisher's advertised supply of 1,750 copies was soon exhausted, and out-of-print book dealers began to raise their prices. Suddenly a new supply appeared on the shelves of new-book retailers at the regular price of $8.50, and the word got around that a West Coast book wholesaler had returned a large part of his 200-copy original order to the publisher, who could then supply his retail customer's backorders. Whether the rumor was accurate or not, the book is now out of print and has been for several years, and fine copies are selling for $25.00 and up in the out-of-print market, with an additional premium for copies of the regular edition autographed by Green.

(C) *The Last Trail Drive Through Downtown Dallas,* talking book edition, by Ben K. Green. Read by Neal Mullins. Talking Books, Adult, 1974. Division for the Blind and Physically Handicapped, Library of Congress, Washington, D.C. 2 R APH. TB 4328. Obtainable on a loan basis only, from the Library of Congress through local, regional and sub-regional libraries for the blind. The entry in the catalog of books available for the blind (obtainable, among other sources, from the Texas State Library, Austin) describes the contents of *The Last Trail Drive* as follows: "A yarn-spinning, old-time horse trader and veterinarian recounts a boyhood adventure. He tells of taking all his savings and heading for a ranch near San Angelo, Texas, where he bought 120 horses at $7.00 each, which he sold for a great profit en route home. 1971." Actually, of course, Green tells of driving the horses to Bossier City, Louisiana, across the Red River from Shreveport. There he held a private auction, sold all his horses but one, and took the train back to his home near Greenville, Texas, selling his last horse to the station agent for $10.00 as the train pulled out.

The recorded version consists of two 10-inch black plastic disks (four sides), designed to be played at 16 revolutions per minute on special portable phonographs furnished free of charge to the blind. In the center of each side there is a light blue paper label. On sides 2 and 4 the label carries the following information, printed in black:

TB 4328
Ben K. Green
The Last Trail Drive
Through Downtown Dallas
On 2 Records   Side 2 [4]
Pages 1–37
Read by Neal Mullins
Copyright 1971 by Ben K. Green
By permission of the publisher
Northland Press
APH 112021
16 RPM

The reverse of each side carries some information in Braille, together with the following printed notice:

Recorded 1972 for
The Library of Congress
by permission of the
copyright holder
By the
American Printing House for the Blind
for special distribution as

authorized under
P.L. 89–522

Each record slides into a paper protective envelope, and the two records are housed in a cleverly designed one-piece plastic mailing carton substantial enough to withstand almost any amount of rough handling from the postal service.

The reading by Neal Mullins is clear, undramatic, and completely free of accent. The first sixty seconds of the recording provide the listener with a brief sketch of Green's career, omitting any reference to study at Cornell University or in England. Then the story begins: "When I was riding past Hamilton's filling station and garage on a pretty good kind of a sixty-dollar horse, etc." Although no regional accent is discernable in the reading, Mullins, obviously a professional reader, does not attempt to correct Green's grammar, and the "hickese," as Richard Bosse once termed Green's writing style, comes through very well. No reader, however, could match the flavor of Green's own oral story-telling style, and Mullins wisely does not attempt to do so.

[Compiler's note]: The publishing history of *The Last Trail Drive Through Downtown Dallas* began, for me, one day in the Spring of 1970 during one of Green's periodic visits to my bookshop. In the course of our conversation he said he had another story in mind about the time when, as a kid, he had driven a bunch of half-wild horses through Dallas, and he asked me if I thought it would sell. Having read his other stories, I of course said it would, and that I would be glad to order a number of copies when it came out. I had occasion to write him in May about the special leather binding he had commissioned for a copy of *Horse Tradin'*, and in my letter I find this paragraph: "On thinking it over, I believe your idea of publishing the story of the "Last Trail Drive Across North Texas" is great, and you ought to be dragged through a cactus patch if you don't do it. I feel it ought to be published first as a separate story, like *The Shield Mares.*" Apparently he received similar encouragement from other sources, for the book was published the following year by Northland Press, as noted previously.

A most interesting account of the publication of *The Last Trail Drive* appeared in *Arizona Highways,* in the issue for October 1971, (vol. 47, no. 10), on page 32. The article, entitled "Northland Press and the Fine Art of Bookmaking," by Paul E. Weaver, publisher, utilizes this story of Green's to illustrate the processes through which an author's manuscript goes before it appears in print. Excerpts:

> This book was sheer fun all the way and combined every element which is indigenous to our scale of operations and our part of the country. The author, Dr. Ben K. Green of Cumby, Texas, had been introduced to me through mutual friends at the Cowboy Hall of Fame in Oklahoma City. . . . When I first visited him at his office in Greenville, it was to discuss his book, *The Color of Horses.* [Eventually published by Northland several years later in 1974.] During the visit he mentioned another manuscript, which he had tentatively titled *The Last Trail Drive Through Downtown Dallas,* and we then talked about the possibility of my publishing it in a limited printing. Well, Ben Green is a damn funny guy and a most successful storyteller, so I was very anxious to read this West Texas yarn of his boyhood horse-trading experiences.
>
> From the first reading I knew this was a wonderful story for Northland Press and I could already visualize it as a fine little book. After simple, but firm contract negotiations (Ben's a tough, wily old codger), the editing of the manuscript was started by our editor Doris Monthan. Now, some manuscripts are difficult, take considerable rewriting, checking, researching, and general reorganization; but in this case, it was flat simple. Ben writes exactly as he saw it, and that ends it, as Doris soon discovered on her first meeting with the seasoned author. Only two minor

changes were recommended and both were shot out of the saddle by a brief, but eloquent lecture on West Texas dialogue from author Green. Ben writes with a full command of the era in which the story takes place, and the manuscript demanded illustrations which created the same feeling and authenticity which Ben had caught in his words.

The person I thought of immediately was friend and well-known Western artist, Joe Beeler, who lives just a good lope from here [Flagstaff] in Sedona. I gave him the manuscript, and after a few days, checked back to see how he felt about it. As I anticipated, he thought the story fun and said he'd really enjoy doing the illustrations and working with Ben. The final acceptance of all illustrations for the book was up to Ben, so Joe did a preliminary sketch. In many of our books, particularly the [Western] art books, we work very closely with the author from the original concept through most of the planning, editing, and design stages. When we presented the sketch, Dr. Green expressed not only satisfaction but downright enthusiasm, so Joe went ahead with the illustrations and we were one more step down the trail.

With an edited manuscript and finished illustrations in hand, I then worked very closely with our designer, Robert Jacobson, to actually set on paper a working layout of the visual ideas suggested by the story and illustrations. We decided on the type face, the deposition of space as to margins, color combinations, paper, and binding cloth — all with an eye to general harmony and suitability to the book's theme. In this case we aimed at an earthy, rustic quality, choosing coarse-textured brown cloth for the cover, textured gold end sheets, and off-white laid text paper. We chose sepia and black for the two ink colors, using the black for the type and combining it with the sepia to achieve greater depth and tonal variation in the illustrations. Also, the sepia tones seemed to suggest the period and general area of the story.

Publisher's Weekly gave the book a send-off with an advance review [quoted from below] and a reproduction of one of the illustrations. They fastened on the very quality we were hoping to achieve throughout the planning of the book: "A warmly appealing bit of nostalgic Americana, enriched by some fine authentic illustrations. . . ." It was the beginning of an actual bombardment of great reviews, and to top it off, it was just our luck to finally hit the best seller list with a limited edition. *The Last Trail Drive Through Downtown Dallas* was in the top ten of the Fort Worth–Dallas area for weeks, and for a while it was second only to *The Sensuous Man,* which shows even Texans have more than one interest.

REVIEWS OF LAST TRAIL DRIVE

Publisher's Weekly, March 1, 1971. A brief unsigned review under "Forecasts, Non-Fiction," indicating that the book is scheduled for publication on April 1, 1971. The reviewer says:

"The yarn-spinning old-time horse-trader and veterinarian saunters back to his boyhood experience when he took two horses and all his savings, bade his Pa goodbye, and rode 250 miles southwest to a ranch near San Angelo, Texas, where he'd heard good Texas ranch horses could be bought cheap. Buying 120 horses at $7 a head, he hit the trail back home with two hired men, a Choctaw Indian, Choc, and an older Mexican, Friole. Green's tale is an understated, droll and flavorsome recital of their experiences, which included driving their herd of unbroken horses through downtown Dallas in the days of Model T Fords and selling them en route at great profit. A warmly appealing bit of nostalgic Americana, enriched by some fine authentic illustrations by Joe Beeler."

The Dallas Morning News, Monday, May 3, 1971. Review by Paul Crume in his front page column "Big D." He says, in part:

"It may not have been the last trail drive through downtown Dallas, but it sounds as if it might have been. This happened years ago when Green, a brash kid, was moving about 100 head of horses from the Paint Rock country, where he had bought them for $7 a head, to East Texas, where he planned to sell them for many times that. . . .

"There are some who say that Ben Green can take a small story and make a big one out of it. That is a yarn spinner's privilege. His tale is a delight."

Forty-Four Range Country Books Topped Out by J. Frank Dobie in 1941 and Forty-Four More Range Country Books Topped Out by

Jeff Dykes in 1971. The Encino Press, Austin, 1972. Design by William D. Wittliff. 32pp., brown cloth, thin octavo. Limited to one thousand copies signed by Dykes.

My good friend and fellow bookseller Jeff Dykes selected forty-four cattle country books published since 1941, which he considered worthy to be added to J. Frank Dobie's earlier list of important range books. Among the new forty-four he lists *The Last Trail Drive Through Downtown Dallas,* commenting, in part:

"This is a delightful true story of the author's teen-age adventures as a big-time horse-trader. Green bought 110 horses from a Paint Rock, Texas, rancher and drove them via Brownwood, Bluffdale, Tolar, Granbury, Fort Worth, Dallas, Rockwall, Mineola, and Marshall to Bossier, City, Louisiana, trading and selling all the way. The foul-up on the Dallas–Oak Cliff viaduct was a dilly, but it was by no means the only humorous happening on the summer-long drive.

"The book is enhanced with drawings by cowboy artist Joe Beeler and Northland Press provided expert printing and an attractive format. There are those who will argue that this is not the writing Vet's best book and the truth is that he is the most entertaining of the current story-tellers of range life. . . . You can't go wrong with Green."

Persimmon Hill, vol. 2, no. 1, November 1, 1971. Published by the National Cowboy Hall of Fame, Oklahoma City. Review, on page 39, by Don Hedgpeth, editor. Excerpts:

"I've come across another book lately that I would like to mention. It is cut from the authentic Western fabric and smells of horse sweat and saddle leather. Unfortunately, it was published in limited editions and is probably already unavailable by the time this gets into print. . . .

"The high point of the story comes when young Ben, with his Mexican cook and the half-breed cowboy called Choc, attempts to drive the horses through the middle of the business district of Dallas in mid-morning traffic.

"To go along with the story are six fine illustrations by Joe Beeler. Joe can do things with horses besides just paint them and his pictures are as much a part of the story as the author's dialogue. *The Last Trail Drive* is the kind of a real story that disproves the widely held opinion that cowboying died out with longhorn cattle. And Ben K. Green, himself, is proof positive that there are still range country men around of the same mold as those who trailed cattle from San Antonio to Abilene in 1867."

The Last Trail Drive Through Downtown Dallas has also received reviews or notice in the following:

The American West (magazine) September, 1971. A brief six-line notice.

Arizona Horseman, August-September, 1971. Review by Carol Marston under "Horseman's Library."

Books of the Southwest, no. 160, June, 1971. Brief note.

East Texas Historical Journal, ____, 1971. Review by Frank H. Smyrl.

Old West (magazine), Winter, 1971. Review entitled "A Modern Classic" by the Old Buckaroos.

Fort Worth Press, Sunday, May 9, 1971.

San Antonio Express-News, July 25, 1971. Review entitled "Humor on the Trail Right Through Dallas."

The Westerner (magazine), August, 1971. Reviewed under column "Books of the West."

¶ 17 *A Thousand Miles of Mustangin'.* Northland Press, Flagstaff, Arizona, 1972.

Octavo, 9¾ inches tall by 7¼ inches wide, 145pp, published in: (A) a first trade edition; (B) a limited signed deluxe edition; (C) a second printing of the trade edition published in December 1972; and (D) a third printing of the trade edition issued in June 1976. All editions are illustrated by Joe Beeler.

(A) First trade edition. The first trade edition is bound in binder's linen of the color of German, i.e., dark, mustard, with a flat back on which the title is stamped lengthwise in gold: "A Thousand Miles of Mustangin' — Green." A prancing mustang 2¾ inches tall is stamped in gold on the lower stuff that we weren't used to, so we had a feast for a few days, but I had begun to worry about my money and was trying pretty hard to do some horse business.

There was a whiteheaded old cowboy came down to the stock pens one day and walked through my horses and visited, drank a cup of coffee and said he would like to have a good young horse

A Thousand Miles of Mustangin'—Joe Beeler illustration on page 129

right front cover. The endsheets are dark gray, and are pasted directly to the half-title at the front, and to the colophon page at the back. Headbands of brown and yellow cord decorate the top and bottom of the spine.

Collation is as follows: Page [i] half-title; [ii and iii] double title-page; [iv] copyright page reading:

Copyright 1972 by Ben K. Green
All rights reserved
First Edition
ISBN 0-87358-098-2
Library of Congress Catalog Card Number 72-76378
Composed and Printed in the United States of America

[v] blank except for Green's "Syringe and G" brand in light brown at the upper right corner; [vi] blank; pages 1 through 145, the text; page [146] the colophon, reading:

A Thousand Miles of Mustangin'
Was set in 12-point Aldus
And printed on Mountie Warm White Text
Bound at Roswell Bookbinding in Phoenix

The dust jacket is of orange paper with the title of the book printed in red, and the Joe Beeler drawing of a cowboy on a prancing horse — like that on the title page — printed in black. The back side of the jacket contains a later photograph of Green sporting a grizzled, almost white, beard, an open shirt collar, and his usual Western-style hat. Although he wears a faint smile, he looks much thinner and older than in the somewhat baby-faced portraits of his earlier books, showing the effects of his bouts with diabetes and pneumonia which, as he said, "damn near carried me off."

(B) The limited edition. The limitation page, on laid paper rather than the wove of the text, is tipped in between the free front endsheet and the half-title. It reads:

Especially bound
and limited to 150 copies this
de luxe edition
has been signed by both
author and illustrator
No. ____
[Signed in black ink]
Joe Beeler
Ben K. Green

The special binding consists of a bright red imitation-leather spine extending nearly half-way across the covers, the remainder of the covers being in a dark brown closely woven binder's linen. The endsheets are of red paper rather than the dark gray of the regular edition, and the book is boxed in a substantial cardboard slipcase covered in dark gray paper, with the silhouette of the prancing mustang stamped in gold on the front side of the box.

Collectors partial to leather on their expensive limited edition bindings may question the publisher's selection of red fabricoid instead of calf or morocco for the spine, but perhaps the original signatures of Joe Beeler and Doc Green on the limitation page will make up any deficiencies in this regard. The limited edition is noted by my friend Jeff Dykes in his *Fifty Great Western Illustrators,* on page 9 (item No. 43 under *Beeler*).

(C) Second printing of the trade edition. A second printing of the trade edition was issued in December of 1972. It is identical in all respects with the first trade edition, with the exception of the words "Second Printing" in the copyright notice.

(D) Third printing of the trade edition. The third printing of the trade edition of *A Thousand Miles of Mustangin'* is, internally, identical with the editions described above, with the exception of the words "Third Printing — June, 1976," in the third line of the copyright notice. Externally, however, it differs from them in several respects. The new edition is bound in a khaki-colored cloth of a coarser weave than the binder's linen of the earlier printings, and the end-papers are a rich brown rather than dark gray. The paper of the dust jacket is a strong red-orange, as compared to the paler orange of the earlier jackets. Somewhat surprisingly, no change has been made in the text of the biographical sketch of Green on the rear flap; it still recites that "Doctor Green does his writing and raises fine horses on his ranch near Cumby, Texas," with no mention of his death in October, 1974.

[Compiler's comments] From the collector's standpoint, both the limited and trade editions are handsome, well-printed volumes, with both typography and editing of high quality throughout. Point-hunters will note a misprint, "He wondered if *I he* could catch him and look in his mouth," which occurs at page 130, line 11, in all editions. It should also be noted that a sizable excerpt from the book (comprising pages 92 through 105 of the text) was reprinted in *The Quarter Racing Record* issue of December 15, 1973, beginning on page 226, under the title "Wild Mustangs and Yaqui Indians."

Many Green *aficionados,* including myself, regard *Mustangin'* as his most entertaining book, and in some respects his most self-revealing. Green recounts his adventures as a solo hunter of wild mustangs in what was at that time (the 1930s) the wilderness country of the Texas Big Bend and the mountains of northern Mexico. He makes friends and helpers of the lonely wandering Mexicans and the primitive but fun-loving Yaqui Indians whose customs and folklore were described so well by another venturesome Texan, J. Frank Dobie.

For a year he lives in the open, eating the native foods:

frijoles, tortillas, and wild game; stalking, lassoing and taming the fleet mustangs (he was told at the beginning that there were none, and he would be chasing only phantoms). Once he nearly loses his right hand from an infected horse bite; the wound is cured in a week by an old Mexican medicine-woman (*curandera*) who applies a paste of wheat flour and sourdough yeast — "Here was the making of penicillin in its first and crudest form, and I was too dumb . . . to recognize what the old medicine-woman knew would cure infection." The *capitan* of a band of Mexican rangers stops the trail herd and demands a properly signed *permitir*. "From the bottom of my saddlebag I brought out . . . a U.S. $20 bill which was a gold certificate and one side was gold colored. He turned it over a time or two and felt of it and I asked, '*Capitan,* is it made out right and in proper order for you to accept?' 'Si, senor,' and he folded it and stuck it in his vest pocket and waved his men to let the horses go."

The special charm of this book, I think, derives from Green's description of his encounters with the denizens, both human and animal, in a part of the world unfamiliar to most of us (as it was unfamiliar to him, too). In *Horse Tradin'* and his other books Green encounters people to whom *we* can relate either by experience or vicariously: Vermont maids, rival horse traders, Southern colonels, schoolmarms, Texas stockmen, *et al.* But here, in dealing with people of a kind unknown to him, he displays the possession of a personal trait for which there is no adequate term in English. But the Hispano-Americans call it, simply, "*Simpático.*"

REVIEWS OF A THOUSAND MILES OF MUSTANGIN'

Abilene (Texas) *Reporter-News,* November, 1972. Review by George Near. He says:

"*A Thousand Miles of Mustangin'* is the longest single story

Green has published to date, and good as it is it suffers in comparison to his shorter yarns. He describes a Depression-era jaunt into the wild Big Bend country to corral some wild mustangs people have heard about but no one has ever seen. The episode proves to be the toughest one of his career, and he finally finds the 'phantom' mustangs, although what he planned to be a month-long trip turns into a year's journey from the time he stayed in Jenks Magee's mule barn in Abilene until he finally returns home."

Austin (Texas) *American,* November 30, 1972. Long review headlined "'A Thousand Miles' Traces Mustangin' in Big Bend Area," by Carol Sutherland Hatfield, Special Writer. Excerpts:

"Ben K. Green might not be the funniest yarn spinner in this country. My memory serves me correct that Mark Twain was no inferior storyteller. But I have it on good authority that he's the funniest one in Texas to come along in a good many years.

"As a Texan who recognizes a good 'Texas' yarn and who has told one or two on occasion, Green is unsurpassed in his ability to tell his audience those little observational details of human attributes and events, with just a mite touch of exaggeration, that make up a good story. . . . And for this very funny, colorful story of looking for wild mustangs in the Big Bend Country at the tail end of the depression, Green is being honored this year at Writer's Roundup. He will be in Austin for the award-winning ceremonies, which begin with a dinner at 7 P.M., December 2. . . .

"*A Thousand Miles of Mustangin'* is one of his longer stories about a jaunt into the Big Bend to corral mustangs for future sales, since he 'had about used up all the hard ways to make a livin' ahorseback.' Drifting on south into Mexico, he survived a number of adventures before reentering the U.S. west of Nogales, Arizona, with a large herd of horses he managed to capture with the aid of Yaqui Indians.

"Anyone who's familiar with Big Bend Country and with that wildly beautiful section of the Rio Grande River can find heartwarming references in Green's book. . . .

"Green's writing style is casual and spontaneous, the way one tells a story to friends. Another passage from the book: 'You don't make a good outdoor man until you quit carrying a watch and lose track of the days by not having a calendar. Then time ceases to be of any particular importance. You go to bed when it's dark and get up when it's daylight and eat when you get hungry and suppose it's the right time of day.'

"But what's best about Green is not that he's a writer, but that he really knows what he's talking about."

A Thousand Miles of Mustangin' was reviewed widely around the country, as evidenced by the following list:

Boletin Bibliographico, no. 481, January 1, 1973. A Mexican government publication. Review entitled "Mil Millas en Caballo Cerrero," Mexico City, D.F.

Arizona Daily Star, December 3, 1972. Review by Dave Brinegar entitled "A Thousand Miles — A Lot of Country, A Lot To Tell About."

New Orleans Times Picayune, Sunday, February 11, 1973. Review by Ernest G. Fischer entitled "Trainer Tells How to Catch Wild Horses."

Nashville Tennessean, February 11, 1973. Review by Carl May entitled "Wrangler Has Fine New Yarn."

Leisure, February 25, 1973. Review entitled "The Real West," by Philip C. Freshwater.

Western Horseman, February, 1973. Short review in "Bunkhouse Bookshelf" column.

Houston (Texas) *Chronicle,* April 1, 1973. Short review entitled "Ben Green Tells More Tales."

Sun Day, Cheyenne, Wyoming, May 6, 1973. Review, unsigned.

Wichita Falls *Times,* Texas, May 6, 1973. Review entitled "Yarns by Top Hand," by Henry W. Barton, in Magazine Section.

East Texas Historical Journal, Fall 1973. Review.

Arizona Living, November 24, 1972. Notice of an autographing party for Green and Joe Beeler, reading: "You're invited to drop by and meet the renowned yarn-spinner, horse trader, and author, Dr. Ben K. Green, at a cocktail and autograph party for his newest Northland Press book, *A Thousand Miles of Mustangin'*. Joe Beeler, Arizona's fine Western artist from Sedona, illustrated the book and will also be present. Main Trail Galleries, 7169 Main Street, Scottsdale, Arizona 85251. 6–8 P.M., Friday, November 24, 1972. Informal.

Dr. Green will be happy to autograph any of his books you may already have."

[Compiler's note] In *How Come I Wrote a Book,* one of the volumes in *Ben Green Tales,* Green tells of his frustrations and failures in trying to do his own marketing of *Horse Conformation [and] Hoss Trades.* As a result, he was quite willing to cooperate with his publishers in attending autograph parties arranged by them with numerous bookstores around the country after he had become famous. But the strain of meeting the deadlines of appearing at two or three stores in the same city on the same day was hard on him, perhaps harder than we knew. For example, on one occasion he had agreed to come by my bookshop for a visit after an autographing session in Dallas at Cokesbury Book Store and Doubleday Book Shop downtown. When he didn't show up, I called Bill Gilliland at Doubleday. He said that when Ben finished the session there, he was so tired that he just wanted to be driven home to Cumby, and had already left. Having seen Ben not long before, I understood.

¶ 18 *Some More Horse Tradin'.* Alfred A. Knopf, New York, 255pp. First published September 14, 1972. Issued in (A) "advanced proofs, uncorrected," for review copies; (B) regular trade edition, first issued in bright green cloth, later in chocolate brown cloth; (C) a limited edition, boxed; and (D) recorded on *Records for the Blind.*

(A) The Advance proofs, uncorrected. This is an odd-shaped book, 11 inches tall by 5½ inches wide, and 15/16 of an inch thick. It contains 202 printed pages, numbered by hand in ink, and is bound in green paper wrappers with Knopf's orange title-label fastened to the front cover with scotch tape. A limited number of copies were sent to selected newspapers across the country, so that book reviewers could have their reviews ready by the publication date, listed tentatively as August 18, 1972. Internally, the book contains only the text; there are no illustrations and no preliminary pages.

Some More Horse Tradin'—frontispiece by Joe Beeler

(B) The regular edition, first issue. The title page is worded as follows:

Ben K. Green
SOME MORE
HORSE
TRADIN'
Alfred A. Knopf New York 1972
Illustrated by Joe Beeler

The binding of the *first* issue of the trade edition was a very bright green cloth, with a saddle and stirrups stamped in gilt on the front cover, and the title in two lines of gilt on the spine. For the second and later issues the cloth was changed to a chocolate brown, much more compatible with the tan dust jacket. The gilt stamping remained unchanged.

The copyright page, p. [6] contains 16 lines of information of the usual kind, but includes for the first time in one of Green's books the "Library of Congress Cataloging in Publication Data," reading, in part:

Green, Ben K. *Some More Horse Tradin'*.
1. Horse buying. 2. Horses — Legends and stories.
I. Title. SF301.G744 636.1'08'I 70–38336
ISBN 0–394–46123–I. First edition.

These numerical codes are no doubt designed for computer manipulation in an information storage and retrieval system for libraries.

The book contains 255 numbered pages. Collation: Pages [i, ii, iii] blank; [iv] "Also by Ben K. Green," etc.; [v] half-title; [vi] full page charcoal drawing of two mounted cowboys, by Joe Beeler; [vii] title page, as above; [viii] copyright page; [ix–x] contents pages; [1] half-title, repeated; [2] blank; [3] title page for first story, "Runaway!"; [4 and 5]

first page of text, with Joe Beeler drawing of young cowboy seated on ground, with his horse tethered behind him; pages 6 through 255, the text with the page numbers omitted on the title page and first page of text for each of the 15 stories in the book; page [256] blank; [257] A Note About the Author; [258] blank; [259] A Note on the Type; [260–262] blanks.

The dust jacket, designed by Lidia Ferrara according to a note on the back flap, is of buff laid paper printed in dark brown and maroon. A subtitle on the front cover reads, "More Great Yarns from the author of *Horse Tradin'*." The blurb on the front flap deserves some notice. Unlike the blurbs on the dust jackets of his other books published by Knopf, which are relatively literate and restrained in tone, this one throws all such restraints to the winds, and in an unfortunate attempt to imitate Green's style, tries to entice the buyer with such gems as:

> From the same corral that produced the widely loved *Horse Tradin'* Ben "Doc" Green has rounded up 15 new [!] yarns filled with the ornery yet irresistible "con" that has branded Doc's books as classics of Western Americana. *Some More Horse Tradin'* recounts the go-arounds [!] of Doc and a whole slew of craggy old-timers and rangy characters. . . . See all of them matching their wiles and hear a lot of palaver, dealin', and tradin' for well-bred usin'-type mares, snorty-like range horses, and even used-to-be bad horses from the tumbleweeded plains of Texas to the mountain meadows of Yankee Vermont. [!] So here you go — with Doc Green and his horse-tradin' West in finest fettle." [Wow, podnuh!]

Aside from this, the front flap gives the price of the book as $6.95, and states that it is "Illustrated with sixteen line drawings by Joe Beeler." The rear flap contains the bob-tailed biographical sketch of Green, eliminating the references to Cornell University and the Royal College of Veterinary Medicine. The first printing of the dust jacket is dated "9/72" at the bottom of the back flap, and the back of the jacket is entirely taken up with the pensive portrait of Green used on the other Knopf book jackets.

There is a misprint (wouln't for wouldn't) in the next to last line of the second full paragraph on page 11.

(C) The limited edition. The limitation page reads as follows:

> Of the first edition of
> SOME MORE HORSE TRADIN'
> three hundred and fifty copies have been
> printed on special paper and specially bound.
> Each copy is signed by the author
> and numbered.
> Ben K. Green
> [Signed in black ink with felt-point pen]
> No. ____

The limitation page is printed on heavier paper stock than the text pages, and is tipped in at the front immediately following the free front endpaper.

The book is bound in natural (very light tan) buckram with a dark green buckram spine heavily decorated in gold. Green's Syringe G logo is stamped in gold at the center of the front cover.

The front and rear endpapers are a deep orange-yellow, and the top edge of the pages is stained a light yellow-green to match the yellow and green of the head and tail bands. The fore edge is uncut, causing an irregular surface resulting from the deckle-edge on the paper and the varying widths of the gatherings.

The book is boxed in an attractive cardboard slipcase, which is covered in the same orange-yellow paper used for the end papers. Both sides of the box contain a printed panel extending from top to bottom. Within this are reproduced six of the drawings from the text, done by Joe Beeler, printed in light brown ink.

(D) [Recording] "Some More Horse Tradin'," by Ben K. Green, read by Charlie Pyle. Talking Books — Adult, 1974. Division for the Blind and Physically Handicapped, Library of Congress. 3R. APH. No. RD 6055. "Recounts western adventures with craggy old-timers and colorful characters including a watermelon hauler, an undertaker, and Will Rogers, the public cowboy. 1972." The foregoing description is taken from the current catalog of Talking Books published by The Library of Congress, Washington, D.C. The record I saw had been obtained on loan, without charge, from the Texas State Library, Austin, Texas, in a special mailing carton. Presumably it would be also available by ordering from other state or local libraries which participate in the Talking Books Program. At latest report, none of Green's writings are available on tapes or cassettes.

[Compiler's comment]: A true bibliographer is not supposed to have, and indeed is proscribed from, a concern with the quality or content of the material under examination. But I confess that should I be forced, under duress of gunpoint or hurricane, to choose only one of Green's books to be marooned with on a deserted island, I should select *Some More Horse Tradin'*. Besides containing a reprinting of *The Shield Mares,* which many critics and readers consider his masterpiece, and its close runner-ups, *Texas Cow Horses and the Vermont Maid* and *The Last Trail Drive Through Downtown Dallas,* it includes the charming *Cindy,* with its ending reminiscent of O. Henry at his best, and a number of other excellent yarns. It would not suffice as the only book, but it would be excellent company over a long haul, and there are few books today which could claim as much.

Fort Wayne, Indiana, *News-Sentinel,* October 14, 1972. Review entitled "Horse Tradin' Yarns Spun," by Georgia K. Kaufman.

" 'The Old Gray Mare Ain't What She Used to Be' would be a good theme song to go with this collection of fifteen short stories about horse tradin'. Although the subject of horse trading is a little antiquated for a current book, perhaps cowboys and horses and the love of the West will always be popular. . . . Ben K. Green spins some mighty entertaining yarns which happened about the time the automobile was becoming popular. But no one thought anything would take the place of the horse."

As an indication of the growing popularity of Green's writings, and, incidentally, of his colorful personality as good literary "copy," reviews and notices of *Some More Horse Tradin'* appeared in the following papers:

Amarillo, Texas *News,* September 21, 1972. Review by Steve Cornett entitled "Horse Sale Tales From Trader Doc."

Abilene, Texas (date not known). Article by George Near entitled "Two New Books Out by Ben K. Green."

Austin, Texas *Citizen,* October 26, 1972. Review (includes also *A Thousand Miles of Mustangin'* entitled "Visiting Author Tells of Villages in Rural Travels."

Nashville, Tennessee *Banner* (date not known), 1972. Review entitled "Green Again on Horse Tradin'."

New Orleans *Times Picayune,* October 8, 1972. Review by Ernest G. Fisher entitled "Tradin' Horses Was His Game."

Pittsburgh, Pennsylavnia *Press,* October 27, 1972. Review by Wyndle Watson.

Richmond, Virginia *News-Leader,* September 27, 1972. Review entitled "Some More Tales from Southwest."

Sacramento, California *Bee* (date not known). Review by Philip C. Freshwater.

¶ 19 *The Quarter Racing Record,* Fort Worth, 1972–73. Three stories by Green in separate issues, as follows:

"Runaway," a reprint of the first story in *Some More*

Horse Tradin', published in the issue for January 15, 1972.

"Strong Medicine," one of the stories in *Village Horse Doctor: West of the Pecos,* in the issue for January 15, 1973.

"Wild Mustangs and Yaqui Indians," an excerpt (comprising pages 92 through 105) from *A Thousand Miles of Mustangin',* in the issue of December 15, 1973. This excerpt deals with that part of the book in which Green negotiates with the elders of a tribe of Yaqui Indians in the northern mountains of Old Mexico for their help in rounding up wild mustangs. He gets along fine with them, and is mightily impressed with their ability (especially that of the girls) in doing the round-up on foot. An editor's note states that this reprint is made with Green's express permission, and provides a summary of the first part of the book leading up to the adventure with the Yaquis.

℄ 20 *Rhoads West: Wild Western Humor,* by Fred Rhoads. Foreword by Ben K. Green. Northland Press, Flagstaff, Arizona, 1972. Green has written a brief two-page "Foreword" to this book of raunchy cartoons by the creator of "The Sad Sack," and the collaborator in the comic strips "Beetle Bailey," and "Snuffy Smith." Excerpt from the "Foreword": "I have been known to be a darn hard critic when it comes to anything about horses, be it in the flesh, the written word, or painted on canvas. In an awful lot of cases I feel my criticisms have well been justified. Too many artists make a horse look humorous, though unintentionally. Fred Rhoads makes humorous horses, funny people, and laughable cartoons. He's intentional."

℄ 21 *O S Ranch Steer Roping and Art Exhibit, 1973.* Post, Texas, September 29–30, 1973. Edited by David and Ruth

Ann Newby. "Artists' biographies by Ben K. Green—Greenville, Texas."

(A) Regular edition, 8½ inches tall by 11 inches wide, 90 pp., white plastic spiral binding, white stiff paper covers, with a color reproduction of a Tom Ryan painting, *Sunday Afternoon,* on the front cover, and a bronze and wood by Jim Hamilton entitled *Early Trainin'* on the back cover. This handsome official catalog is printed throughout in black and red on buff paper.

The brief biographies of the thirty-two exhibiting artists were compiled by Ben K. Green, in part, presumably, from personal interviews. As a former practicing veterinarian, Doc Green had little use for Western artists whose works displayed ignorance of correct horse conformation. He was forthright in condemning such errors, and did not hesitate to lambast the artists who committed them. In fact, one or two of the biographical sketches had to be rewritten before they could be used in the catalog. Green's ideas concerning the artistic portrayal of horses in Western paintings are stated, in characteristic prose, in the following quotation from his signed introduction to the sketches, appearing in the catalog on page 20:

> It is my personal opinion that there is no place in Western art for impressionistic painting, or any other sort of technique that might be used to camouflage, deceive, or grotesquely portray any of God's handiwork. My principal interest in . . . Western art is to "ride herd," so to speak, on the modern artists that don't know and in some instances, don't care, about my friend, the horse, and how he should be reflected to coming generations. I am brutally frank, seldom misunderstood and didn't take Carnegie's course. It is my custom to express my exact opinion without modification or doctoring concerning Western art, and I'll never be noted the most popular man at an art show, but if my efforts cause some artist to wipe off his paint brush, scratch his

brow, reset his glasses and put more detail and authenticity in his work, then I'll feel well paid for my efforts. Ben K. Green.

Pages 86 and 87 of the catalog contain a montage of the photographs taken during the 1972 Steer Roping and Art Exhibit. In the lower left corner of page 86 there is a 3 by 3-inch photo depicting Doc Green having a friendly chat with Western sculptor Frank Polk. Green's biographical sketch of Polk, on page 39, reads, in part:

> Frank Polk is an old boogered-up cowboy that has set lots of broncs and handled thousands of cattle, both the good and the bad kind. The reason that Frank Polk's sculpture is exactly authentic is because he has lived every buck, jerk and movement that he molds into bronze and if somebody doesn't understand something about one of his bronze pieces, it is because they are ignorant and not because Frank hasn't got it exactly right.

In the lower left corner of the 3 by 3-inch photo there is a postage-stamp sized picture of Green holding a copy of his book, *Some More Horse Tradin'*.

Incidentally, the Post, Texas, *Dispatch* for October 10, 1964, carried a short obituary on Doc Green's passing, quoted in full in Part III of this bibliography.

(B) Special edition, limited to 100 copies bound in leather, for the officers and directors of West Texas Boys Ranch, San Angelo, Texas. The Boys Ranch is supported, in part, by the proceeds from the O S Ranch Steer Roping and Art Exhibit.

(C) The 1975 Program of the O S Ranch Steer Roping and Art Exhibit was dedicated to "Dr. Ben K. Green." Page 4 of the Program contains a large oval photograph of him in his dress-up clothes, white hat and string tie, and with a smile on his bearded face. Below the photograph are two paragraphs quoting excerpts from his introduction to the artists' biographies he wrote for the 1973 Program. The dedication page was sponsored "Compliments of First National Bank, Post, Texas."

¶ 22 *Ben Green Tales.* By Ben K. Green. Northland Press, Flagstaff, Arizona. No date, but copyright by Ben K. Green 1974.

This is a set of four cloth-bound books, tall thin 8vo, measuring 5 by 8½ inches, boxed in a black cloth slipcase with a white paper label reading "Ben Green Tales / by Ben K. Green" printed in dull green and black, pasted on the cloth to the right of the open end. Spine titles are stamped lengthwise in gold on each volume.

Volume 1 of the set is entitled *When I Was Just a Colt.* It contains 57 pages, bound in green cloth, and is illustrated with five pen-and-ink drawings by William Moyers, whose biographical sketch appears on page 57 of the book. The endsheets are in olive-green paper. This volume (1) furnishes the bibliographical information and limitation detail for the entire set. The limitation page reads:

Ben Green Tales
This special edition
of four boxed, deluxe-bound volumes
has been limited to 1,250 sets
signed by the author.
[A list of the volumes and illustrators]
This set is number ____
[Signed diagonally from bottom to top]
Ben K. Green

Volume 2, entitled *Up Fool's Hill Ahorseback,* is bound in dull yellow cloth, with the title page printed in buff and black. It contains 79 pages, with endsheets of burnt orange paper. It is illustrated with five pen-and-ink drawings by John

Volume 1 of *Ben Green Tales*—William Moyers illustration on page 29

Hampton, whose biographical sketch appears on page 79. The book recounts some entertaining escapades of Green and a school-boy *compadre* very appropriately nick-named "Trouble." Ben himself, of course, is called on to rescue Trouble and his several victims from their predicaments.

Volume 3, entitled *Beauty,* is bound in blue cloth, and is illustrated with six pen-and-ink sketches by Joe Beeler, whose brief biography appears on page 59. The reasons for Green's affection for his favorite horse are adequately presented in this book. On several occasions Beauty saved both his life and his reputation as a cowboy.

Volume 4, entitled *How Come I Wrote a Book,* is in some respects the most interesting of all. The five illustrations are by James Boren. The book contains 51 pages, in which Green tells his side of a long-continuing "cold war" waged against what he regards as bumptious or uninformed females in the television and publishing businesses, beginning with his famed tilt with Ms. Barbara Walters over whether, in reading from one of his books, he said "nigger," "Negro," or "nigra," on NBC's *Today* program. He also has much to say, mostly uncomplimentary, about the business ethics of the publishing industry generally. As entertaining as this is (at least to those readers not in the industry), strictures on morals and honesty coming from an old-time horse trader can perhaps be taken with more than a grain of — well, salt, and a harking back to the pot's calling the kettle black.

REVIEWS OF BEN GREEN TALES

Weekly Livestock Reporter, Fort Worth, Thursday, April 25, 1974. Review, unsigned, entitled "Mental Therapy, Texas Style," in the column "Stuph & Thangs." Excerpts, preserving — reluctantly — the original country-phonetic spelling:

"There was a groop of us normally malcontent fellers settin' around th' Livestock Exchange Bildin' th' other day. . . . Someone says, 'Where the heck is ol' Doc Green hidin' out, he ain't been around here in a long, long time?'

"Nobuddy seemed to have seen Doc fer a long while, which in some cases is considered lotsa luck, but one of th' boys figgered Doc was either writin' another book, or was busy on the banquet circuit complainin' about how someone had served peas without smashed pertaters . . . and someone else figgered maybe the rubber chicken had done him in at last, and we went on to other important matters.

"We finally give up and went back to th' offis to take up what we smilingly refer to as work, and Lo & Behold! Here was a package from Greenville, Texas, from Doc Ben Green, and bless his heart he had sent us a set of his newest books published by Northland Press called *Ben Green Tales*. . . . We read 'em nonstop, and discovered that Doc ain't lost none of his talent fer spinnin' Texas tales with all th' artistry that Chet Byers used to spin the lariat rope. . . .

"We felt kind of brainwarshed as we meandered down th' old trails with Doc, sort of like we had sent our brain out and it come back nice and laundered.

"We finally figgered that stuph like Doc Green writes is sort of therapeutic. While we don't pertend to be able to perscribe nuthin' for nobuddy, we recommend a little of Doc Green's kind of medicine for anybuddy. Git a copy of one of Doc's books, or this latest set of four little *Ben Green Tales*. It'll git your mind off your problims as effectively as havin' a horse step on your pet corn. Thanks, Doc, see you soon, I hope."

Arizona Daily Star, April 14, 1974. Unsigned review entitled "Horse Expert's Set Published."

Books of the Southwest No. 189 for April–May, 1974. Short unsigned review.

The Chronicle of the Horse. Unsigned, undated review.

❡ 23 *Money on the Hoof — Sometimes,* by Edith Wharton Taylor. Introduction [by] Ben K. Green. The Old Army Press, Fort Collins, Colorado, 1974. 115 pp. plus "Acknowledgments" page.

(A) Trade edition. The binding is brown cloth in pictorial dust jacket, orange endpapers. Printed on buff paper, with many photographs of the old Fort Worth stockyards and the stockmen who owned and operated them. The title page contains a fold-out leaf which provides a triple page spread for the book's title. Green has written a brief one-page Introduction, dated March, 1974. He states, in part:

> The author has portrayed the development of the livestock marketing industry in the North Central Texas area with special attention given to the developing of the Fort Worth Stock Yards and packing houses. . . . This research material has been brought alive by interviews with several of the surviving livestock operators who were there when the Fort Worth Stock Yards was in its infancy. Much of this material would never have been brought to light and put in print had it not been for the painstaking efforts of the author and those who contributed their knowledge and experiences.

Trading compliments, the Acknowledgments page contains the following thanks to Green for his help, along with thanks to others who have contributed information:

> Special gratitude is due Ben K. Green for his expert knowledge of the subject, his careful scrutiny of this book, and his helpful criticisms. The author wishes to thank Dr. Green most gratefully for permitting tapes to be made of his interviews with men involved in the marketing of livestock at Fort Worth.

On page 61 of the text there is a brief note concerning Green, reading in part:

> Ben Green went to work at the Fort Worth Stockyards when in his teens. His job was to use his keen eye for conformation and size of livestock, and sort and group cattle into lots that would be most acceptable to a potential customer. But his principle [*sic*] interest in the livestock industry has always been in horses and mules. Before he turned twenty, he was driving herds of horses

and mules from West Texas to the Fort Worth horse and mule market. . . .

On the reverse of page 64 there appears an unusual photograph of Ben Green as a young man, dressed in a conventional business suit, with coat, vest, dress shirt and tie, striding along the sidewalk in downtown Fort Worth. The picture bears a caption reading:

> On the day I was twenty-one years old, I shipped some fat steers to the Fort Worth market that brought $5.10 a pound [but see the entry under B below] and weighed 1,060 pounds. It was such a good price and such good weight that I decided to dress up and take in the town. Ben K. Green.

(B) Special edition, signed by Edith Wharton Taylor and by Green, limited to twenty-five copies, and offered for sale by Fred White, Jr., Bookseller, as item 858a in his catalog no. 22, Bryan, Texas, no date [1976]. This is the regular trade edition in dust jacket, but with a transparent acetate wrapper around it, and boxed in a substantial slipcase covered, somewhat incongruously, in brown marbled paper. In the catalog note to the item White states:

> This edition came about when I requested that the publisher, Mike Koury of The Old Army Press, have them sign these copies for me. He did and they were shipped just prior to the Western History Association annual meeting in Rapid City. Dr. Green died on the way back from South Dakota. I then had a slipcase prepared along with a limitation page.

The publisher's account differs somewhat. Mr. Koury states that he shipped twenty-five copies of the trade edition to White in Texas from the Old Army Press in Fort Collins, Colorado, and that he, Koury, had no further connection with the matter. White's recollection is that when the books arrived he delivered them to Green, who signed them and had

Mrs. Taylor sign them on the back of the title page. White then had a special limitation page printed, reading:

Limited to 25
autographed copies
of which this is
number ____

The limitation page, blank on the reverse side, is tipped in just ahead of the page signed by Mrs. Taylor and Green which, as we have noted, is the back of the title page. This is a matter of some importance to the collector of signed limited editions, since it indicates that the signers inscribed their names on original copies of the book itself, rather than on separate sheets of paper which were later pasted into the book after publication, a practice frowned on, if not actually condemned, by true bibliophiles. It should also be noted that while the text is printed on a buff-colored *wove* paper, the limitation page is printed on *laid* paper, in which the "ribbing" shows, like a watermark, when held to the light.

In all copies of the special edition examined, the caption to the youthful picture of Green on the back of page 64 has been corrected in black ink (by Green himself according to Fred White). The word *pound* has been lined through, and "100wt" (hundredweight) inserted in its place, making quite a difference in the amount of money Green received for his steers. So far as I can determine, this correction was not made in the regular trade edition copies, with the possible exception of a few copies Green might have peddled personally during the Western History Association meeting at Rapid City, South Dakota, just prior to his death.

❡ 24 *The Color of Horses. The Scientific and Authoritative Identification of the Color of the Horse.* With Paintings by

Darol Dickinson. Northland Press [Flagstaff, Arizona, 1974]. [Logo].

[On copyright page]: "Copyright 1974 by Ben K. Green. All Rights Reserved. First Edition. ISBN 0-87358-131-8. Library of Congress Catalog Card Number 74-79459. Composed and printed in the United States of America." Square 4TO (10 by 11 inches), 127 pp.

(A) Trade edition. Issued in dark forest green cloth, with Green's Syringe G logo in gold at the upper right corner, and with black endpapers at front and rear. The spine bears the legend printed vertically in gold reading as follows: "Dr. Ben K. Green, The Color of Horses, Northland Press."

The book is printed on heavy coated white enamel paper, with the verso of page 127 blank. The dust jacket, printed on heavy white coated stock, reads: "Dr. Ben K. Green / The Color of Horses / The Scientific and Authoritative Identification of the Color of the Horse / With 34 full-color paintings by Darol Dickinson." Preceding the last line are six full-color reductions of horse pictures from the book. The back of the dust jacket is blank except for Green's logo in gray at the upper right corner.

The front flap of the dust jacket carries some interesting information. After announcing the price of the book at $25.00, it continues, in part:

> This is the first definitive book on the color of horses. Dr. Ben K. Green has taken the research of thirty years and created an easily-read and well-documented book on how color occurs and can be identified in horses. . . . The differences in opinion concerning horse color are widespread, and since horse enthusiasts are independent-minded people, this book may not settle all arguments. But it will certainly provide a standard definition of all colors for those who are interested. . . . Dr. Green began his research in the 1940s in the Trans Pecos region of West Texas

[where] 'there was an array of colors unmatched anywhere else in North America.' He also studied horses during his travels in South America, Europe and the Middle East. . . . This handsome book is destined to become the standard reference on color at every racetrack, farm and ranch in the world.

(B) Limited edition. From the limitation page: "A Deluxe Edition of one hundred fifty copies of *The Color of Horses* has been specially bound, numbered and slipcased. Each copy has been signed by the author and the artist. This is No. ____." All copies I have seen have been signed in black ink, "Dr. Ben K. Green / Darol Dickinson."

Internally the "deluxe edition" is identical with the trade edition, except for the limitation page, which has been tipped in (i.e. pasted in) on a stub between the front endpaper and the half-title. The limited edition is bound in black buckram cloth, with the spine in green-and-black leatherette, stamped in gold like the trade edition. The substantial slipcase is covered in black buckram, unadorned except for Green's Syringe G brand in gold on the upper right corner of the case.

From the book-collector's standpoint, this is the last book actually signed by Doc Green for his publishers. The signing was done very shortly before his untimely death, and a very short time before the book was actually put on the market. In fact, both the regular and limited editions were published posthumously, which leads to the following comment:

Ben Green told me on one of his visits to my shop: "If and when I die, this book on Horse Coloration [his idea for the title] is what I expect to be remembered for by horse people. I've been working on it for more than twenty years, and it's the only scientific study on the subject that I know of." He also said that he had made numerous color photographs of sample horse-hides over the years, but that color values on photographic film were so unpredictable as to be worthless in

DR. BEN K. GREEN

THE COLOR OF HORSES

The Scientific and Authoritative Identification of the Color of the Horse

With 34 full-color paintings by Darol Dickinson

The Color of Horses—dust jacket

reproducing the actual color of horses, and it would take a real artist, like Darol Dickinson, to get printed representations of what he was trying to portray.

(C) The Color of Horses Calendar, 1975. From the book *The Color of Horses: The Scientific and Authoritative Identification of the Color of the Horse,* by Ben K. Green. Northland Press, Flagstaff, Arizona, 1974.

This is a handsome calendar for the year 1975, issued in 1974 as an advertising piece to announce the forthcoming publication of Green's *The Color of Horses.* The calendar, 9¾ inches tall by 10¾ inches wide, is bound at the top with spiral plastic. It contains 12 leaves (24 pages), with the reverse of each leaf bearing a fine color painting of a horse by Darol Dickinson, one for each month. The months and their horses are as follows: January, the Blood Bay; February, the Grey Three-Year-Old; March, the Bright Chestnut; April, the Seal Brown; May, the Grulla; June, the Palomino; July, the Buckskin; August, the Raven Black; September, the Liver Chestnut; October, the Coal Black; November, the Light Bay; and December, the Standard Bay. The reverse of the December page is blank.

The front cover is of coated heavy white paper stock, bearing the picture of the Liver Chestnut horse reduced in size to 4¼ by 3½ inches; its reverse side is blank. The following page serves as the title page, and is headed "From *The Color of Horses. The Scientific and Authoritative Identification of the Color of the Horse,*" followed by a seven-line description of the forthcoming book. Beneath this description there are two short columns of text, with pictures of Green and Darol Dickinson, with the left hand column containing a brief sketch of Green and the right hand column containing a sketch on Dickinson.

The calendar exists in two states, because of some changes

requested by Green in the wording of the title page and because of some revisions desired by Northland. In the first state, the description of the book ends with the statement that "This long-awaited book will be published in October. Price $25.00." In the second state the publication date reads "October, 1974." In the first printing the sketch of Green begins, "The Author: Ben K. Green is a man who has *been around* horses all his life. . . ." At Green's request the wording was changed to read, "The Author: Ben K. Green is a man who has *worked with* horses all his life. . . ." An outsider may well wonder whether the difference is sufficient to justify a reprinting of the entire page. Again, in the first state Green's sketch ends with the sentence, ". . . his work has produced the first definitive book on the subject of color." In the second state this reads, ". . . his dedicated work has produced a valuable book and a beautiful calendar."

Northland Press advises that only forty-seven copies of the calendar in its first state were bound up, these being for Ben's use and for Northland to distribute during the gathering of the American Booksellers Association in Washington, D.C., in June, 1974. From a collector's viewpoint, the possessor of one of the first state calendars would have a rare Ben Green ephemera indeed!

REVIEWS OF THE COLOR OF HORSES

Dallas Morning News, Sunday, February 23, 1975. Review by Frank X. Tolbert entitled "Ben Green's Finale: On Color of Horses." It reads, in part:

"Doc Green lived to see what he considered his most worthwhile contribution to the horse culture, the one for which he had researched most of his adult life, come off the presses. However, he died on a highway in Kansas before the actual publication date in December of *The Color of Horses.*

"Ben Green's pride is illustrated with oil paintings by Darol

Dickinson of a dark bay Thoroughbred who 'favors' a stud on Green's ancestral ranch near Cumby, Texas, and a light bay Arabian, and a standard brown Morgan, and a native-bred dun, and a grey Percheron who resembles Jeff, a stallion on Doc's ranch, and a number of other horses of various colors. The paintings are in full color, naturally.

"Doc completed his *magnum opus* under stress. In his last years he was in poor health; a heart attack, diabetes. To add to his misfortunes in 1972 his team of matched Percherons, hitched to a Studebaker wagon, 'just took a notion to run away.' Ben had a hard fall, from the springy seat of the wagon, landing on his forehead. Ben doctored himself. After the accident he told me:

" 'I was already hip-sweeneyed, bowed in the tendons, and troubled with cinch sores. And now I got a hole in my head.'

"I first heard of the book called *The Color of Horses* when Ben and I were riding around his horse pasture about two-and-a-half years ago. We stopped to gaze on a beautiful black filly, called April for the month of her nativity, an April the result of a romance between the Thoroughbred stallion and a grey Percheron mare. Although big-boned, 3-month-old April didn't have the heavy feet and barrel-like legs of her mamma, and Doc said he bred her for a 'hunter,' or fence-jumping horse. She would be larger than her papa but symmetrical.

" 'She'll be a beautiful black mare,' I said. 'Only she won't be black as an adult. She'll be grey like her mamma,' said Ben. It was then that Doc told me of the arduous research he had done through the years on the hair and hide of horses to determine what made color.

"Doc's book will be a controversial one. He says he researched for it all over the world, including some time spent with Arabs, in Middle East deserts. 'By laboratory techniques I learned how to extract the pigment from the hair and from the dermis tissue. After a year of extracting pigment from horses of various colors, I was convinced by my findings that there is only one pigment that colors all horses,' he writes in the Introduction to the book.

" 'It was in the third year of research that I began to understand that it is the arrangement pattern of the pigment in the shaft of the hair and the density of the pigment that refracts the lights and reflects the color that is identified by the human eye as being bay, chestnut or any other color.'

"Doc said he split some 4,000 horse hairs, 'and each color treated in this book will show the pigment refraction pattern that causes a certain color or shade.'

"The book isn't all a chronicle of laboratory research. There are the usual Ben Green brand of 'tales' about horses."

Outdoor Arizona for February, 1975. Full page article by Don Dedera entitled "The End and Beginning of Arguments." Excerpts:

"Four hundred and thirty-five years [after Coronado] a reference book exists to settle once and for all the lively disputes which have raged since the first human slipped a vine noose around the neck of the first bronc. The new authority is *The Color of Horses,* by Dr. Ben K. Green. The publisher is Arizona's own Northland Press of Flagstaff. [Paul Weaver] accepted the manuscript of a thoroughly opinionated veterinarian who had begun assembling knowledge as a boy after the turn of the century. In the 1940s, Dr. Green used his far-ranging practice to gather up hair and hide samples which he scrutinized in his specially equipped laboratory.

"He literally spent the mature years of his life splitting hairs. He found that for all the colors of horses there is but one pigment — a dark amber substance which he extracted and analyzed. Along with his manuscript, Dr. Green submitted enlarged sketches of exactly how pigment is arranged for various kinds of refraction patterns that cause colors and shades.

"A less imaginative publisher might have opted for photographic illustrations. Paul Weaver instead commissioned a young but acclaimed artist, Darol Dickinson, to render thirty-four magnificent oil paintings. Then, with everybody kibitzing, the paintings were lovingly transferred to Northland's exacting color press.

"The resulting illustrations afford dimensions beyond the practical grasp of photography. The thirty-four pictured horses have perfect color, are ideally conformed and combine an interesting mix of breeds. Never, in Europe, or New England, or the American Southwest, or anywhere else has there been a reference which succeeds in setting the standards for identifying horse color.

"'What we've done,' says Weaver, 'is to produce an historical first . . . we've had the guts to tell the world that from now on, *this* is a blue roan, *this* is a buckskin, *this* is a liver chestnut, *this* is a blood bay; and dammit, if you don't agree with us, go split your own ten thousand hairs and paint your own pictures and print your own book."

"Alas, Dr. Green is not present for the controversy. As the book was nearing publication, he died, quite gray."

Arizona Horseman for October–November, 1974. Review entitled "New Book on Horses Bright, Informative."

El Paso Times, Sunday Magazine for December 19, 1974. Reviewed in "Book Briefs."

Arizona Republic, for January 3, 1975. Thirteen line review.

Books of the Southwest, no. 195, November, 1974. Short review.

The Western Horseman, January, 1975. Two-column article.

Hammond, Indiana *Times,* February 2, 1975. Seventeen-line review.

Spokane, Washington, *Daily Chronicle,* Thursday, February 13, 1975. Article by Elvetta P. Lewis, two columns, entitled "Truisms Exploded."

Arizona Republic for January 5, 1975. One paragraph article in Sunday section by Carol McNaughton, under "New Titles."

Fort Worth Star-Telegram, Sunday, January 19, 1975. Feature story by Leonard Sanders entitled "Horses, Texans Receive Attention of Publishers."

Rocky Mountain Quarter Horse, for January, 1975. Article entitled "Darol Dickinson Illustrates Latest Book by Dr. Ben Green."

Clark County, Nebraska, *School District Newsletter,* vol. 6, no. 4. Review by Ken Bowers.

Newsletter No. 10, Brislawn-Edwards Wild Horse Research Farm, February, 1975. Article on Ben K. Green, praising *The Color of Horses.*

¶ 25 *Arizona Highways* for January 1975, vol. LI, no. 1., pages 2 through 9. This issue of the magazine contains a reprinting of approximately three-fourths of "Insight into Horse

Color," Green's long introduction to his book, *The Color of Horses*. There are six color reproductions from the book, of which one, on page [4] of the magazine, is a handsome color photograph of Doc Green in his Sunday-best clothes, wearing a bright smile with his whiskers. It should be noted that the *Arizona Highways* article also reprints the final chapter of *The Color of Horses,* entitled "Spots, Paints, Piebalds, and Appaloosas," in which Green gives just over one page to a discussion of parti-colored horses.

The editor of *Arizona Highways* has added a brief comment to accompany Ben's portrait mentioned above. He says, in part:

> There may be someone more qualified to write *The Color of Horses*—there may be—but as Dr. Ben once remarked, "He ain't been born yet." Ben K. Green in his lifetime traded, raised, treated and used more types and breeds of horses than anyone else we know. . . . Ben Green died of a heart attack . . . on his return to Texas from Rapid City, South Dakota, where he had attended the Western History Association Convention. Prior to leaving Rapid City, Ben told friends he felt "Like he was just about rode out." We loved Ben despite his . . . "incredible amazement at the sheer brilliance of our ignorance" . . . regarding horses.

Part 2

GENERAL ARTICLES ABOUT BEN K. GREEN

AS THE READER will have discovered by this time, Doc Green was an intensely colorful character. He was picturesque in appearance, salty in language, and unique in vocation — an irresistable combination to any journalist, no matter how blasé, who happened to come under the spell of his picaresque personality and gift of gab. But he had, especially in his mature years, a serious side, that of a dedicated scientist bent on educating his fellow veterinarians in the field of toxicology, and his fellow horse-lovers in the proper handling of horses. This dichotomy between the man of science and the storyteller is evident in his first book, *Horse Conformation [and] Hoss Trades of Yesteryear.*

That he had another side, that of a rollicking good fellow, and (no less) a singer of cowboy songs, appears from the following excerpts from page 49 of John A. Lomax's *Adventures of a Ballad Hunter* published in 1947, quoting a letter from Tom Hight, the old-time cowboy singer of California:

> I sang [in a singing contest] against a fellow in Weatherford, Texas, in a wagon yard. His name was Ben Green. His and my friends done the matching of it for a quart of whiskey. So we had quite a jolly time, about thirty men, and they sure got a kick out of it. I beet him in about three hours. He said he had never been beet before.

It appears that in a cowboy singing contest, quantity, not quality, was the aim; the contestants sang alternately until one could sing no more, having run out of songs or breath, or both, so that the last man to sing was the winner. Lomax does not give us the date of Tom Hight's letter, but Hight himself indicates in other passages that the event took place some years before. Since Lomax's book appeared in 1947, we may assume a date in the late 1930s, perhaps, while Ben was a resident of Weatherford. The quotation from Hight also appears in *Cow Camps and Cattle Trails,* a reprinting of a portion of Lomax's works published by the Encino Press of Austin, Texas, in 1966.

In the years during and following World War Two, Green practiced as a veterinarian in the horse, cow and sheep country of Texas and New Mexico, with his headquarters in Fort Stockton and San Angelo, Texas. Here he was involved with technical problems of livestock feeding, many of them described in *Village Horse Doctor: West of the Pecos.* A few press notices from this period of his life have survived, and are cited and quoted from in the first items below, these being, so far as I am able to determine, the first references to Green and his work to reach the dignity of print.

The San Angelo *Standard-Times,* Thursday, April 10, 1947. Long article headlined "New Era (?) For Sheep. Sutton Flocks Do Well On Weed With Medicated Feed," by Al Sledge, *Standard-Times* staff writer. Excerpts:

> Sonora, April 9. Two sheep-feeding experiments which show possibilities of opening a new period of development in the sheep industry were visited near here today by a small but highly interested group of producers from more than six West Texas counties. The experiments have been the feeding of sheep, old crop lambs, and yearling ewes . . . in pastures having nearly 100 per cent coverage of bitterweed — a range plant which has forced many ranchmen to liquidate their entire flocks.
>
> The Fields brothers — Bill and Herbert, Ozona, and Gus Wheat who ranches east of the ranch experiment station in Edwards County, cooperated with Dr. B. K. Green, Fort Stockton, in the experiments. The sheep are fed a special medicated mix-

ture prepared by Dr. Green. . . . The Fields, Wheat and some others say the feed did the job; preventing the sheep from becoming ill and dying because of eating bitterweed. They are convinced the sheep thrived on the medicated feed and bitterweed.

Some are doubtful; they do not believe the medicated feed will work; they do not believe it is the answer to the bitterweed trouble which is spreading each year and today covers a large part of the sheep range, forcing many ranchmen to turn entirely to the production of cattle and goats.

Bill Fields was mighty skeptical over the proposal to feed the lambs in the bitterweed trap. Herbert wanted to try it, and together he and Green talked Bill into the idea. . . .

Dr. Green explained that he ran some forty-six tests before he hit upon what he thinks to be the right formula. He says the drugs in the feed are not injurious to the sheep, but that a ranchman should not endeavor to feed this mixture to sheep which are already sick from bitterweed. It won't work, he says, since the drug serves as a preventive and not as a cure.

"The bitters in bitterweed is what makes the sheep eat the plant," Dr. Green says. "In order to get the sheep to eat this special feed one must put the feed in a pen. After a sheep is taught to eat, he'll come after the feed any place it is put in the pasture. Bitterweed 'experts' tell me that sheepmen can get by without much ill effect in their flock if they have some relief to carry them from sixty to seventy-five days in the spring. I believe these two experiments have proven this medicated feed will get the job done."

Before taking on the bitterweed experiments Green ran some tests on yellow weed, which is found in the range country around Fort Stockton. . . . Green says the yellow weed and bitterweed are cousins in the weed family, but the yellow weed is the more potent. He says he has isolated the toxic content of both weeds.

Dr. Green has two other feeding experiments under way on bitterweed. One is at the Hamlin Elrod ranch near Sterling City and the other at the ranch of Steve Calverly, Jr., Garden City. The quantity of consumption of the medicated feed will depend entirely upon the demand, he said. Drugs used in the feed, he reported, are not plentiful and he has had some trouble in obtaining sufficient supplies for these experiments. Ranchmen from Tom Green, Edwards, Schleicher, Val Verde, Crockett, Sutton and Pecos Counties visited the two Sutton ranches today and inspected the flocks.

Fort Stockton (Texas) Pioneer, Friday, April 18, 1947. "Sheep Doing Well After 70 Days on Bitterweed In Experiment at Sonora with Green's Feed." The article states:

> Interested ranchmen from a wide area of West Texas last Wednesday inspected two Sonora projects in which the effectiveness of a medicated feed is being tested as a preventive of the toxic effects of bitterweed on sheep.
>
> The sheep in two projects have been fed seventy and sixty days respectively, with a medicated feed developed by Dr. Ben K. Green of Fort Stockton, first as a preventive for the toxic effect of the yellow-weed which grows in portions of the Trans-Pecos.
>
> Believing that similar treatment might counteract bitterweed trouble, Dr. Green arranged for . . . tests at the Sonora ranches of Bill and Herbert Fields and Gus Wheat. . . .
>
> Bill Fields in relating the story of the experiment to *The Pioneer,* stated that he was at first skeptical of the project, but was talked into it by his brother, Herbert, formerly a vocational agricultural teacher in several Texas schools. Results fully justified his brother's faith, he says, and next winter the feed will be tried on all the ranch's sheep, except those in one pasture as a test. . . .
>
> Dr. Green, in commenting on the experiments, emphasized that the medication is a preventive, and is not recommended as a cure for animals already affected by toxic effects of either weed. . . . Biggest problem now facing Dr. Green is the securing of sufficient supplies of drugs used in the . . . feed preparation.

Also from this period is the following advertisement, obviously written by Green, and published in a sheepman's trade journal, probably in April, 1947.

SPECIAL FORMULA FEED
Is Not Expensive to Use . . .

One ton of feed contains 4,000 doses of special formula — and cost of medication is only 1.2¢ per head, per day, plus basic market cost of protein feed.

Bitterweed is a nutritious feed, provided its toxic effects are counteracted by the use of special formula feed.

Anticipate your future needs and write or call

DR. BEN K. GREEN
Phone 8
Fort Stockton Texas

The Shamrock, Fall 1967, published quarterly by The Shamrock Oil and Gas Corporation, Amarillo, Texas. A major biographical article on Green by Tommy Kelley, editor, entitled "A Lifetime A'horseback," with many direct quotations by Green that did not appear in his subsequent writings. Excerpts:

> "I have been in the horse business all my life," Green says, "and I'll be in it when it's over. You know, few men have stuck to this business . . . and I consider it quite an accomplishment to have made a living from it during the advent of the machine age.
>
> "First Monday, Country Trades Day, that was when the farmers brought in something they didn't want, to trade to somebody else for something they didn't want, both of them with the full intention of cheating the other," Green recalls. From this early introduction to the business transactions of the times, Green learned many of the ropes that were to help him successfully conduct his career as a horse trader.
>
> Green recalls that his family had an indirect part in naming the city of Greenville where he spent some years of his childhood. "There were three families of Greens settled where the town is located today. My people came there in 1834, two years before the Republic of Texas was formed. My great-grandfather traded

with the Caddo Indians and operated a freight line from Jefferson to Fort Worth.

"There was a fellow named Arkansas who worked for the family . . . that's all the name we knew. One day Arkansas brought in a load of freight, and in those days that was the signal for everyone to come in and pick up their supplies. So while everyone was in town, it seemed as good a time as any to hold a meeting. The meeting was in a grove of trees, about where the courthouse is now. Old Arkansas was drunk, but he got to his feet and grabbed a low limb to steady himself, and made a motion to name the town for the most people there by the same name. So they named the town Greensville. Later, the legislature took out the "S". . . . And that's the true story on how the town got its name, despite the claims of those who say it was named for General Green," the good doctor proclaimed.

In pursuing his studies of veterinary medicine, Ben Green conducted research over vast areas of the world, including Australia, South America and Africa, in addition to much of the North American continent. On one such research jaunt involving a botanical toxicology of African plant life, Green realized a narrow escape from death. "We were traveling up the continent, camping every hundred miles or so, and moving any way we could . . . trucks as far as they would go and then by pack animals," Green recalls. "We had a staff of eight and as many natives as we needed. We contacted [*sic*] some type of fever and four of the men died. I got awful damn sick, but never had to go home."

Green helped to finance his veterinary studies by working as an auctioneer in horse sales throughout the country. One such sale provided Green with one of his favorite experiences. "It was in Gillette, Wyoming, back in the days of the Depression," he recalls. "We had horses penned everywhere and started selling in carload lots. By the end of the day we had sold 10,008 head of horses . . . and that's one hell of a lot of horses. There is no hill big enough to hold them, nor is the human eye big enough to see that many horses at one time. And the hell of it was, they sold for an average of $21 a head."

This occasion was recalled by Green several years later when, in Lexington, Kentucky, he watched as George Swinebroad, renowned horse auctioneer, established a new horse record for total receipts in a horse sale. The per-horse average for one hundred head amounted to something over $27,000. "I told George he wasn't so damn smart," Green exclaimed. "I said, Hell, you have sold the least number of horses for the most money. I have sold the most horses for the least money."

Green, over the years, has developed a keen sense of memory and learned to store most pertinent facts in his head, a trait that has helped immeasurably in recalling details in his *'Horse Tradin'* yarns.

Despite a normal degree of attraction to the fairer sex, Green somehow through the years has managed to escape the confinement of "double yoking." In *Horse Tradin',* he relates his youthful infatuation for a beautiful Southern Belle and his narrow escape from the amorous advances of a husband-hunting school marm. But neither managed to get a halter over his head or a ring on his finger. "I always had a 'booger' for that double harness," he exclaims. [Compiler's note: Ben was actually married for a time. The marriage license is of record, but the details of the courtship, ceremony, and (presumably) divorce must await the labors of his biographer.]

Austin (Texas) *Citizen,* October 26, 1972. Article headlined "Visiting author tells of villages in rural travels," by Barbara Lord, *Citizen* correspondent. Excerpts:

"Live, soft-spoken, an' sweet-talkin'; that's the kind of a secretary I use for all my books," grinned Ben K. Green. "I just start a yarn spinnin', and she catches it on paper," he continued to describe his working habits as he autographed his latest books, *Some More Horse Tradin'* and *A Thousand Miles of Mustangin'.*

"Doc" Green, to the delight of his local followers, was hosting an autograph party at Scarbrough's, and it was quickly apparent why his books have a universal appeal — not limited to the folks who admire horse stories. He has lived the life he tells about, and he tells it with good humor and plain language. His love for horses and people (in that order!) is obvious.

Actually it is this love that prompted him to write. He began with simple articles of practical value to horsemen. He threw in a tale or two. Publishers demanded more; so, after a long career as a breeder, trader, and veterinarian, he began writing.

"I've spent a lifetime with horses," Doc Green explained, "I was given a baby colt when I was a year old. Rode away from home when I was twelve, and started wranglin' horses on a chuck wagon in West Texas." It is hardly possible to date his start in the horse and cattle business. [Compiler's comment: It's even more impossible to wrangle horses on a chuck wagon. But maybe Doc was having his joke—or maybe the reviewer had hers.]

The Joe Beeler Sketch Book. By Joe Beeler. With a Foreword by Frederic G. Renner. Northland Press, 1974.

On page 127 of this book of his paintings and drawings, in the chapter entitled "Book Illustration" Joe Beeler comments:

> Catching the character and flavor of the story is very important to me. I have enjoyed working on Ben Green's books from this point of view. Ben gets so much character and grass roots philosophy into his stories that it is a challenge and a pleasure for me to try and do the same. I feel my drawings must try and match his words.

The book contains four of Beeler's illustrations for Green's books, and in three of these Ben himself is pictured as a youngster. The first (on page 118), from *The Last Trail Drive Through Downtown Dallas,* shows young Ben sitting on his bedroll, paying off his helpers, the Indian cowboy Choc and the old Mexican cook Friole. The second (on page 125), is from volume 3 of *Ben Green Tales,* a pen-and-ink drawing showing a self-satisfied young cowboy being fitted by a tailor in a "nice, gray herringbone weave suit." The third (page 126), a charcoal pencil drawing, depicts Ben as a teenager, sitting on the ground with his saddle horse tethered to a post behind him, from *Some More Horse Tradin'*. The fourth, from *A Thousand Miles of Mustangin'*, shows a herd of horses approaching a watering place (on page 127).

The *Sketch Book* also contains, on page 24, what may properly be considered one of the more unflattering depictions of a famous author. It is a pencil drawing of an aging man's bald head as seen from behind, with the back hair reaching down to his coat collar, and with the left ear-piece of his spectacles stretching forward to the front of his head. Beneath the drawing appears Beeler's notation: "Ben Green."

Dallas Morning News, Sunday, December 10, 1972. Report on the Texas Writers Roundup held that year in Austin, by Marshall Terry, Book Critic of the *News*. Excerpt: "Old Ben K. Green, of Cumby, had *A Thousand Miles of Mustangin',* which is one of a bunch of books about horse trading. He claimed he couldn't really write his name [!] but sat in a comfortable chair and told his stories to a pretty secretary, and it sounded like a pretty good way to do it."

Greenville, Texas, *Herald Banner,* Sunday, June 3, 1973. Unsigned article, headlined "Green to Speak At Art Exhibit." "Oklahoma City, Oklahoma — Award-winning author Dr. Ben K. Green of Cumby, Texas, will be the featured speaker Saturday at the eighth annual western art exhibit at the National Academy of Western Art, here. . . . Green . . . is scheduled to speak on a reminiscence of 'The Biggest Lies I Ever Heard.' "

Fort Worth *Star-Telegram,* Sunday, July 1, 1973. Interview with John S. Justin, Jr. and Ben Green conducted by Frankie Paukner, headlined "Western Author Horse Expert. Justin Acquisition Unique." The occasion was the formal announcement of Justin Industries' acquisition of Northland Press, and Justin was asked about Green.

He's a real maverick. . . . When I first talked to him about the merger he candidly blurted, "I don't like it a bit." But I assured him things would be the same and that Paul Weaver would still be running Northland Press.

Paukner then interviews Green:

Green is the first to admit, "I've got an opinion on everything and I don't mind saying so to whoever is listening. . . . Right now, I've been subpoenaed to Ohio to decide if a horse that won a race belongs to the registry papers the owner has presented. If so, the owner will be allowed to take possession of the purse.

Clad in worn Stetson and dark suit, Green defends his knowledge of horses. "I've bought and sold horses in every part of the world except Russia, Japan and China. I've measured with my own little snarly hands and bloodshot eyes 70,000 horses in more than 25 places on their bodies and analyzed bone structure from 110 breeds of horses. I've worked teams in the oil field slush pits, I've used them in building railroads, and I drove a stagecoach in South America with light-boned horses."

With such formidable expertise, he sternly insists that horses are a business, a beast of burden to be put to a particular use. "I do fall in love with some of the ole things. It's not smart, but I do," he admits.

"I was born in Cumby, rode away when I was twelve years old and didn't return for forty years — until enough folks died out and mellowed up that I could return home." At home, he describes his writing technique as "when I pull out the bottom drawer of my desk, put my feet in it and rear back and dictate to my secretary. I write only nonfiction, and when I run out of tales, I'll quit." Green has been described by book reviewers as "a great story-teller."

The East Texan, Student Publication of East Texas State University, Friday, June 30, 1967. An unsigned front page article headlined "Author from Cumby Talks Horses, Horses, Horses."

"There is less knowledge of horses now than at any other time since the Stone Age," Ben K. Green, author of *Horse Tradin',* told an audience of students and faculty here Tuesday. "I've raised, bred and shown more than seventeen breeds of horses. I don't know anything about literature," Green said, "and how I became a literary genius is sort of shocking to me." Green was speaking of his book, which was published recently.

When asked if he had any experience with wild horses, Green replied, "A few million head. I mustanged wild horses in the Southwest United States, lived in the Sahara Desert with Arabs, and bought horses in Montana and Wyoming." While mustanging horses in the Big Bend country of Texas, Green said, to get water he sometimes left his slicker out at night to collect dew. He would lick it off the next morning, he said. Around 1940 he found a herd of pure Spanish horses in Northern Idaho; however they were later killed by forest rangers, he said. "The horse world isn't dead," Green said, "just kind of limited in some places."

The Dallas Morning News, Sunday, November 16, 1969. Article by Frank X. Tolbert entitled "Best-Selling Author Lives in Ranch Shack," in "Tolbert's Texas." Excerpts:

After a long absence, Ben K. Green returned to a little ancestral ranch just north of Cumby, Texas, about seven years ago. "I didn't have a house and I camped on my land for a spell until I found where the cow creatures favored to bed and the horses would go when the weather was the hottest," said Ben K. "And then I built my shack in that mott of bois d'arc trees and oaks where the cool breezes flow. There's a suction of air goes through that grove and it's always five degrees or more cooler than any other shady place around here."

That shack is in a nest of creeks on land patented in 1841 by his great grandfather, David Washington (Wash) Cole, the founder of the City of Black Jack, Hopkins County, later renamed in honor of a politician, Col. Bob Cumby.

You wouldn't be prepared for the shack. . . . If you've read his books you'd suspect that Mr. Green is the kind of a roving

> bachelor who would be happiest in a shack. For he still roams, just as he did in the old horse trading days and when he was a horse doctor in the Trans-Pecos country.
>
> When I stopped off at the Green ranch one day last week, Ben K. had just returned from judging an all-breed horse show in Hawaii. "I found out why those Hawaiians asked me," he said. "I'm the only all-breed judge young enough to travel, and they didn't want to pay the freight on a bunch of judges. I judged one thousand two hundred horses for six days, and luau-ed every night. I was a wreck when I got back to my shack here." Mr. Green asked me to accompany him this week to Waverly, Iowa, where he will be the Percheron judge at the annual Iowa draft horse show and sale. But I had to decline. . . .
>
> The creature on the Green rancho who made the most impression on me, though, is Bluebonnet, a regular poem of a Percheron mare, big as a young elephant and yet shapely as a polo pony. Old Ben K. gave a rebel yell when we were out back of the barns. And Bluebonnet came at the gallop out of the pasture and up to Mr. Green, with high knee action in the thick-grassed meadow and with the comparatively small, Arabian-like head held at a proud angle.
>
> " 'The old Norman knights rode the Percherons' ancestors off to the Crusades and these wonderful horses picked up a leavening of Arabian blood, which is why they're so nimble,' said Ben Green, who once went to the Near East among the sheiks to buy Arabian horses for the Kellogg farms of California."

The Dallas Morning News, November 13, 1967. Article by Frank X. Tolbert entitled "Calling Doc Green On a Crank Phone," in "Tolbert's Texas."

Greenville (Texas) *Herald Banner,* August 27, 1967. Article by Dr. James W. Byrd, professor at East Texas State University, entitled "East Texas Idiom Violates T.V. Taboo," in his column "Views and Reviews." Excerpts:

> It's a well-known fact that Cumby author and horse trader Ben K. Green, at the urging of his Knopf publishers, recently

went to New York and appeared on the *Today* show. What several people don't know, and want to know, is why the network . . . apologized for his "language." You'd have thought that B.K.G. let loose with some old-fashioned East Texas cussin', which just ain't so. I know, "fer I seen and heered it."

He used the local, or colloquial, pronunciation of the word "Negro." He was talking about hoss tradin' in which a "nigger" was involved. He was speaking in his natural vernacular. He didn't say "Negro" for the same reason he didn't say "horse trading" with a speech-professor accent. . . . In short, Ben K. was speaking the language of the Old West and Old South. If his interviewer had read the book she would have known that the author meant nothing derogatory. And a significant point . . . is that the Negro character named William is treated with respect. He may well be the man who is most honest with Green in his horse tradin' days in Dixon, Mississippi."

Eye on the World, by Walter Cronkite. Published by the Cowles Book Company, Inc., New York. Copyright © 1971 by the Columbia Broadcasting System, Inc.

In this book on his experiences as a television newscaster, Mr. Cronkite reports, on pages 290 and 291, an interview with Ben K. Green conducted by Charles Kuralt, CBS's roving reporter for the company's "On the Road" show, "offering looks at people who, in ways both quiet and colorful, demonstrate an American vitality that is our greatest natural resource." The conversation was apparently recorded (no date given) at Green's Pioneer Stock Farm near Cumby, Texas, for it appears in Mr. Cronkite's book in question and answer form. Excerpts:

KURALT: It's been said that if you have any affection for the Old West or a touch of larceny in your soul, or both, you'll get along fine with Ben K. Green. [There is apparently a haitus in the tape here, for Green's response is:]

GREEN: That's the way about horses . . . you'll always have

a few gate and fence problems. They wouldn't feel good if they didn't cause you a little trouble now and then.

KURALT: . . . Where did that little black horse come from?

GREEN: That's a stray. I don't know whose she is or where she came from. She showed up here in the pasture a few days ago.

KURALT: She seems to be eating your oats all right.

GREEN: Yeah, and somebody'll come along in a few days that's missed her. They may have already missed her and realized the grass is good in this pasture, and they'll be a few days finding her.

KURALT: Well, if you were trying to sell me that horse, what would you find good to say about her?

GREEN: Well, I'd say she's a four-year-old, and about fourteen hands high, and would be ideal for a small rider or kid, and she's a nice little short blocky mare with small feet—a pretty good pony, you know, something you'd be proud of.

KURALT: And about how much would you ask for a horse like that?

GREEN: Oh, I'd ask a hundred and a half for her. I think she's worth ninety dollars, but I'd be trying you, you know. I doubt if she's got too much breeding, but I wouldn't have told you that.

KURALT: Now suppose on the other hand you were trying to buy that horse.

GREEN: Well, I wouldn't be trying to buy her, but if I were, I'd say she's long backed and short shouldered, and that her eyes didn't set out on the side of her head good enough, and that she probably didn't have good enough feet to carry her weight, and she had a short hind quarter—and I'd think she's rather a common kind of horse, that would be worth about sixty dollars. Now would you rather I'd buy her from you or sell her to you? Huh?

KURALT: In your long career as a horse trader, did you ever get cheated?

GREEN: Oh, a million times. You get cheated all the time. And it sharpens you up, it's good for you. And while you're getting cheated, you're liable to learn a trick that you can use for maybe more than it cost you. But the man that's never been cheated trading horses didn't trade but once, you know. And that — that adds zest to the deal. You never admit you're cheated, and if an old-timer cheats you, you give him — it gives you a certain amount of respect for him, and you don't get mad at him or raise any trouble about how he cheated you — you file it for future use.

KURALT: Did you ever get stuck with a mean horse?

GREEN: Oh, droves of them, it's easy. . . . And horses are not inherently mean, but they might be inherently stupid, and that makes them mean.

KURALT: That could be a description of some people.

GREEN: Oh, yeah, I know some friends of mine that I could apply that to.

KURALT: How rough was it for a horse-trader in the early days?

GREEN: You had your problems, but it was all fun; it was all fun. And I stayed at it when kids my age were getting them a flivver and stripping it down. . . . But the old men at the wagon yards and the livery stables had what I wanted, and I was referred to as being backwards because I kept some good shod horses, and traded horses, and stayed in the livery stable and the wagon yards when the other kids were up on Nob Hill, you know.

KURALT: No regrets?

GREEN: No regrets. I wouldn't trade a day of it.

The Dallas Morning News, Monday, April 24, 1972. Paragraph in an article entitled "Authors and society mingle," by Sarah Birge, Society Editor of the *News,* covering the private party given by Mr. and Mrs. Fred Smith on the eve of the "Smith College Book and Author Luncheon." The paragraph concerning Green reads:

Mr. Green, a salty sort and a great narrator of his experiences, lives in Cumby and says he's been in the horse business all his life. . . . And even when a team of 'em throws a man like

> Ben Green, he's not down for long. (He explained the gash in his forehead as a result of his being thrown.) Mr. Green was honored Saturday night for two books — *A Thousand Miles of Mustangin'* and *Some More Horse Tradin'*.

Aside from the rarity of the old horse trader's making the society columns of a metropolitan newspaper (an occurrence explainable by the fact that he was never one to shun publicity, regardless of the medium in which it was offered), the article was accompanied by a five-by-four-inch photograph of Green, bearded, bald, and without his hat, seated in a party chair, and wearing a fancy dress suit — somewhat rumpled — with string tie and lapelled vest. Clearly visible on his forehead is a three-inch gash, caused when he was thrown from a wagon when the team he was driving staged a runaway on his farm at Cumby early in 1972. He joked about the incident later, but those who knew him say that he never quite recovered from the effects of the fall.

The Maneater for September 20, 1974, a publication of the University of Missouri, Columbia, Missouri. Article entitled "Ben K. Green; Last Lonely Eagle," by John T. Davis, feature writer, based on an interview with Green at his home ranch in Cumby, Texas.

This is one of the more able and perceptive articles written about Green during his lifetime. Here are some excerpts:

> There are hundreds of towns like Cumby, Texas, scattered across the face of the West; tiny, isolated populations whose vitality is drained every day by the larger cities, and a world of elusive promises. The history and wisdom of these pockets of civilization is guarded by the old men in the cafes and domino parlors and deserted storefronts. In time, generally, that wisdom passes on, to retirement homes and county cemeteries. But not always. . . .
>
> Dr. Ben K. Green is an old man now [He was only sixty-two

at the time]. But in his day — the early years of the Depression and several years thereafter — he was practitioner of every trade that could be followed by a young man on horseback. . . .

His amazing memory for detail covers an unbroken stretch of half a century and the supplanting of one civilization for another.

"I can't explain it," Green said. "It's just something some people are born with, but I have damn near complete recall. An old incident will occur to me and that will suggest other details and it becomes a story when I put it down." He dictates his stories to a live secretary, watching for reactions and furnishing explanations when it becomes necessary.

"You can kill a good story pretty damn quick with too much detail. But I am writing across one or two generation gaps; I need to furnish some explanatory details to carry the story."

The end product . . . is not a conventional "story," but a tale spun before your eyes, the product of a craftsman. To read Ben Green's books or to listen to him talk is to sit before the fire and watch the grandfather everyone should have had raise up a vanished world with the power of his words.

Green's roots in the West go back past his own experiences; he is a fifth-generation Texan himself. "My grandfather opened a trading post in Greenville (Texas) in 1834. And this land I'm living on . . . was paid to another grandfather of mine for serving in the First and Second Legislatures of the Republic of Texas at Washington-on-the-Brazos."

Do people ever doubt that you've lived the times and experiences you write about? (Such as leading a hundred unbroke horses through metropolitan Dallas in the Thirties in a wonder book entitled *The Last Trail Drive Through Downtown Dallas.*)

"Every story I've ever written happened to me exactly as I set it down. Oh, occasionally I get someone who will try to pin me down on such-and-such a detail, but they don't last too long. . . . They're not really tryin' to start an argument, but the Depression and the country were so different from what they know, that's it's difficult for them to believe . . . they can't fathom the era from the standpoint of money — because there wasn't any.

I grew up when the Machine Age was beginning in this country, and kids my age were buying the first flivvers and learning to work in gas stations . . . and maybe a rich man's son had a motorcycle. But even then, my experiences were uncommon. You know, I've never drawn a regular salary in my life. Of course, there were times I'd have eaten a damn sight better if I had, but I've had only myself to answer to. What a person made of himself depended a lot on what the individual was. There ain't many left that can do without. . . . I guess I'm the last of a breed. But I've owned my time."

[Compiler's comment] Doc Green's claim to possessing a photographic memory, or "total recall," has been questioned by many, and he has often been accused of inventing details to color up his stories. I once questioned him myself on the point, being very careful in my choice of words, since if he felt himself insulted by the doubting of his word he would go off with a bunch of "West Texas compliments" like a string of Chinese firecrackers. I must have hit the right note, because he told me that he had cultivated a natural talent for remembering ever since he was a child, and that it had come in very handy in his horse trading days, and later in dictating his stories.

But several decades of legal training have taught me that in dealing with Ben's statements, as with others, it is always good to have some corroboration from outside sources. Such corroboration came to me, out of a clear blue sky, one day during a conversation with my good friend Carter (Tex) Taylor, the veteran owner of the C-Lazy-T ranch near Seymour, Texas, in Baylor County. We were visiting (as Ben would say) in Tex's comfortable home in Fort Worth, and the conversation came around to the subject of Ben Green and his writings.

"I knew him pretty well," Taylor said. "He was considered somewhat of a character around the Fort Worth Stockyards, and almost everybody knew him. One day he came up to me and said, 'Mr. Taylor, you probably don't remember me, but I remember seeing you once many years ago. I was running some cattle on the Brazos down near Granbury. One Sunday afternoon I went over to a nearby girls' camp, where the kids were putting on an open house for their parents. I rode my horse over to the camp, and there was a group of girls gathered around a fellow who was showing off some roping tricks to entertain the kids. I rode up and watched him for a while. You were that fellow. I was that cowboy. We didn't meet then, but I well remember your face and the occasion.'

"I was flabbergasted," Taylor said, "because that incident happened when my daughter, now long married, was a little girl, and my wife and I had enrolled her in the girls' camp for the summer. That must have been at least forty years ago. And I remember that while I was performing for the girls, there was a young man on horseback watching me."

"I asked Ben what he thought of my roping tricks. He chuckled and said, 'Well, I thought you did pretty good for an amateur.' I couldn't let him get away with that 'amateur' business, so I replied, 'Ben, if you can remember me that well after forty years, I guess I'll have to believe about half the stuff you put in your stories.' He chuckled again, and we parted as friends."

Knowing Carter Taylor, I'll accept his testimony in support of Green's claim of near total recall.

Ten Years With the Cowboy Artists of America: A Complete History and Exhibition Record, by James K. Howard. Foreward by Frederic G. Renner. Northland Press, Flagstaff, Arizona, 1976. 213 pp., 4to, bound in navy blue buckram, with title in silver gilt along the spine.

In describing the Cowboy Artists of America 1973 show, held that year at the Phoenix, Arizona, Art Museum, author Howard writes (on page 18, column 2):

". . . The highlight of the weekend was the late well-known author Dr. Ben K. Green. He offered a critique of the artists' work, and in his caustic inimitable style told all of them to depict more action scenes, and quit painting horses which would fall over if they were untied from the hitching posts and fences in the paintings."

Green is also mentioned on page 201 as the author of *The Color of Horses* in the short sketch of Darol Dickinson, a former member of the Cowboy Artists of America, who painted the splendid illustrations for that book.

Catalog, Eighth Annual Exhibition, Cowboy Artists of America, Phoenix Art Museum, September 14–November 4, 1973. Northland Press. 80 pp., stiff paper. Foreword by Senator Barry Goldwater, who wrote, in part: "As for the main speaker of the evening, I not only had the pleasure of hearing Dr. Ben Green, but I sat next to him and was regaled throughout the dinner with his priceless humor on the horse and man's relationship to it."

[Compiler's note: This was the awards dinner held at the same Phoenix meeting of the Cowboy Artists referred to by James Howard in the preceding item.]

Part 3

OBITUARIES

Arizona Republic, Phoenix, November 10, 1974. "Green, author, dies." "Ben K. Green, successful author with Northland Press of Flagstaff and Alfred A. Knopf, Inc., New York, died October 5 in northern Kansas. He was en route from the Western History Association convention in Rapid City, South Dakota, to his Texas ranch when he suffered a heart attack. He was sixty-two.

"Green was often in Phoenix, the last time in September of 1973 when he was the featured speaker at the Cowboy Artists of America Awards Banquet. *The Last Trail Drive Through Downtown Dallas,* now out of print and considered a Southwestern classic was the first Ben Green book published by Northland Press (1971)."

The Sun, Flagstaff, Arizona, Saturday, October 19, 1974. "Western Author Ben Green Dies in Northern Kansas."

Dallas Morning News, October 7, 1974. "Texas Author Ben Green Dies; Rites Wednesday." "Ben K. (Doc) Green, well known Texas author from Cumby, Hunt County [compiler's note: Cumby is actually in Hopkins County, just across the Hunt County line] died Saturday in his car on a roadside near Colby, Kansas. He had been driving from Rapid City, Iowa [actually South Dakota], to his ancestral Hunt County ranch, just east of Greenville, when he was believed to have been the victim of a heart attack.

"Green's books delighted such diverse readers as New York critics, and fullback Walt Garrison of the Dallas Cowboys. A. C. Greene, a Dallas author, said Green 'had the most native ability for writing about his own experiences of any Texas author. And I think he represented the last real voice of old-time Texas in literature.'

"For several years, Green had a severe heart ailment, and friends believe he knew he was about to have a heart attack, pulled the car over on a Kansas highway and died. The car showed little if any damage. Green is survived by a brother."

Dallas Morning News, October 7, 1974. Obituary by Frank X. Tolbert in his column, "Tolbert's Texas," entitled "Requiem for Most Famous Horse Trader." Excerpts:

"Amigo means friend in Spanish. And yet to me amigo has a deeper connotation than friend. Ben K. Green, who died Saturday, was an amigo.

"He always seemed to have about a three-day growth of whiskers. And he was a cow-puncherish old guy of very loud and picturesque speech habits. I think he was careless about shaving and spoke loudly, often with oaths, to disguise the fact that he was really a gentle and cultured man. Just for example he was secretive about being an authority on English bone china.

"Ben King Green was an internationally renowned author. He wrote some of the best books ever about the Southwest. All were derived honestly from personal experiences as a horse doctor and wandering horse trader or as a rancher and cowboy. I think he was the greatest living expert on horses. . . .

"The fact that animals, especially horses, seemed to love Ben K. may be a clue to his personality. His horse herd on his Cumby ranch includes Thoroughbreds and Percherons. His horses would come on call to him and at the gallop. And these beasts, especially the draft horses, are gentle as so many dogs.

"Ben K. Green's uncle, Dr. Ben F. Green of Cumby, died only last month at age ninety. Ben F. called himself 'the senior horse doctor' and with good cause, for he was graduated from the University of Indiana school of veterinary medicine in 1907. Back in September the Rev. Robert Ridley of nearby Campbell, Texas, came to the Cumby cemetery to hold services for his friend, the ninety-year-old horse doctor. Wednesday Reverend Ridley returned to Cumby for the same sad chore, only this time at the services of a sixty-two-year-old horse doctor who happens to be world famous."

Dallas Morning News, Sunday, October 13, 1974. Frank X. Tolbert in "Tolbert's Texas."

"A. C. Greene and I went to the funeral last Wednesday of our friend, Dr. Ben K. Green, the author. Dr. Green was buried in a four-acre pasture adjoining his little ranch on the outskirts of Cumby, Hopkins County, a town founded by one of his great-grandfathers.

"The four-acre pasture also adjoins the old Cumby cemetery, and Ben Green donated the land to the cemetery. Around the grave-site of the author of *Horse Tradin', Wild Cow Tales,* and other best sellers, there was marked off by red flags an area 100 feet by 100 feet. When he donated the four acres to the cemetery Dr. Green stipulated in the transfer of the deed that no one else is to be buried in the 100-foot-by-100-foot area.

"Ben Green once told me: 'I roamed free and always had plenty of elbow room during my span on this earth. And I don't aim to be crowded in after I'm gone.' Dr. Green's grave is in a high-grassed meadow at the head of the valley of a creek and with motts of black-jack oak, cedar, and bois d'arc all round the meadow."

Quarter Racing Record, Fort Worth, November 15, 1974. Obituary headed "Noted Author Doc Green Dies," written by Naomi Scott. Ms. Scott, formerly Naomi Hallum, was Green's first secretary. She did the composition and typesetting for *The Tally Book,* and is credited on the first page of the first edition of *Horse Conformation* [*and*] *Hoss Trades of Yesteryear* with having done the composition for the book. Excerpts:

"He had a serious heart condition for thirty years or more but he didn't let it interfere with his many activities and wouldn't let people know about it until recent years when his health became extremely poor. Still, despite the urging of his friends and relatives to slow down and take it easy, he refused to quit. He worked to the end, writing, taking care of his livestock and traveling extensively to publicize his books and meet lecture obligations, and like most famous cowboys of history, he died with his boots on.

"A rugged individualist, Doc lived simply, even primitively, despite the fame and fortune he gained as an author and lecturer. He spent his last years in what he called his 'batchin' shack' . . . at Cumby. His only source of heat for cooking and warmth was a wood-burning, pot-bellied stove and his bedding was canvas ducking fastened together with metal snaps. Outside horses and cattle roamed, chickens scratched in his yard, lambs grazed in his orchard, and there were pens full of pigeons and rabbits.

"Due to his failing health and the numerous broken bones he sustained during the time he referred to as 'when I was a wild, rough, young cowboy,' he could no longer ride his beloved horses, so he rode around his Pioneer Stock Farm and surrounding countryside in a surrey with red leather upholstery drawn by a spirited bay Standardbred trotting mare.

"His lifestyle was not the only thing that success did not change about Doc Green. To the many people who knew him he was always the same — boisterous, loud talking, saying exactly what he thought, with the sting of his barbed wit not quite hiding the fact that inside he was a gentle, soft-hearted, loyal man who would do anything for a friend.

"Doc chose to be buried in a solitary grave in one of his pastures. It seems a fitting resting place for a cowboy who spent so much of his life sleeping in a bedroll under the stars, with horses and cattle peacefully munching grass nearby."

The Houston Post, Houston, Texas, November 3, 1974. Long obituary by Leon Hale, entitled "Non-writer became man of letters in spite of himself." Excerpts:

"The TLE — Texas Literary Establishment — was a trifle slow about accepting Ben Green. Do you expect it was because he didn't shave and all? Seemed sort of rough? Then there were things in Green's background that people talked about, which I bet pleased him because if you're gonna sell books you need to be talked about. But finally he got all the decorations. Year before last in the Rice Hotel, he was at the head table at the Texas Institute of Letters annual meeting. He stood up in his brown suit and his boots — he still didn't look shaved real good to me but I guess he was — he stood up there surrounded by lacy shirts poking out of tuxedo jackets and he received a special award from the Institute. For his contribution to Texas letters.

"He never called himself a writer. . . . He said he wasn't a writer and he sure was glad because it sounded so blamed hard. He said he never did write anything, he just talked it. Said he had this sweet-smellin', good spellin' secretary to take down what he remembered about his horse swapping and ranching and animal doctoring and trail driving, and all he did was just tell the truth and the secretary straightened up the sentences and put in the paragraphs and the periods, so doing a book wasn't anything but a pleasure.

"Whether Green was really a graduate veterinarian or not doesn't make an ounce of difference to me. Whether he told fibs in his books and passed them off as truth, that doesn't matter either. Lot of people accused him of dressing up his game with details that didn't quite happen. How could a professional horse swapper stick entirely to fact? Ridiculous.

"I am just thankful he passed our way, and did all the talking to that sweet-smelling secretary. In only eight years he left four fine books on my desk. They have yielded much pleasure, and taught me things I didn't know.

"Anyhow Ben K. Green is gone. I thought maybe you hadn't heard about it."

The *Gatesville Messenger,* Gatesville, Texas, October 10, 1974. Obituary entitled "Ben K. Green Dies; Funeral Held Wednesday."

The Herald Banner, Greenville, Texas, Monday, October 7, 1974. Obituary entitled "Dr. Green Dies of Heart Attack." "Dr. Ben K. Green, sixty-two, author and veterinarian from Cumby, died Saturday afternoon of a heart attack near Colby, Kansas. Born March 5, 1912, in Cumby, he was the son of David Hugh Green and Bird Green. Dr. Green studied Veterinary Medicine at Texas A & M, Columbia University and the Royal College of Veterinary Medicine in England. [!]"

Funeral Sermon preached by Rev. Robert H. Ridley, on October 9, 1974, in the funeral chapel at Commerce, Texas. Excerpts:

"Dr. Green was born at Cumby on March 5, in the year 1912. He was the son of Mr. and Mrs. David Hugh Green. His mother was Miss Bird King before she was married to Mr. Hugh Green. He is survived by one brother, John Lee Green, of Gordon, Nebraska, and by his beloved and devoted aunt, Miss Juanita Green, of Cumby. Dr. Green was educated in the South at Texas A & M. He studied in the North and East at Cornell University in New York where he studied veterinary medicine, and he did post-graduate work abroad at the Royal College of Veterinary Medicine in England.

"There were things about him and about his writings which I think he, as an honest man, would not expect us to approve or applaud, but there were things about him and about his writings which we can approve and commend, and of which we should be highly appreciative. He had a brilliant mind which God had given him and which he had developed over the years. He had great ability to deal with details effectively, sometimes throwing light on and adding warmth to the story. He writes, and we are with him by the lonely campfire at night. We accompany him in the great box canyon in the Rockies. We ride with him in the drenching rain. We enjoy with him the hospitality of a plain family in a ranchhouse out in the West.

"In one of his Christmas letters, he called attention to the fact that the Christian meaning and the importance of Christmas were instilled into him at a very early age. He has been represented as being more interested in Christ than in religion — and as one who seemed to sometimes trust the Lord more than he trusted the Lord's disciples.

"The wide-open spaces of Kansas seemed to furnish an appropriate place for him to die, especially appropriate, it seems, that he should meet his Maker all alone — not in the crowded streets, or in the disciplined and regimented environment of the hospital — but in the quiet of the countryside.

[At the grave side] "There is a sense in which — so far as the body is concerned — Dr. Green comes back to Cumby today — back from the Brazos River country — back from the land of the Pecos — back from the high Rockies . . . back from the plains of Kansas."

The *Post Dispatch,* Post, Texas, October 10, 1974. Obituary entitled "Author Ben K. Green dies on Kansas trip." Excerpts:

"Dr. Ben K. Green, that delightful storyteller of another Southwestern generation — and their horses — won't be back at the OS Ranch Art Exhibit next year. The seventy-eight [!]-year-old author died of a heart attack Saturday afternoon en route from Kansas back to his home in Cumby, Texas. . . . Ben, with his whiskered countenance, has been a fixture at all three of the OS Ranch art exhibits and had an autograph party given him in the Post Public Library during his first one. 'We've lost a friend, a very good friend,' Librarian Pee Wee Pierce told the *Dispatch* in informing the paper of the death of Dr. Green. (The doctor title is because Ben was a veterinarian.) Ben was not married and his only survivors, *The Dispatch* has been told, were some distant aunts. On his visit to the library here two weeks ago Dr. Green brought a gift copy of a book, *Money on the*

Hoof — Sometimes, a history of the Fort Worth Livestock Commission and stockyards. He had written an introduction for the book which was authored by Mrs. Edith Wharton Taylor. Maybe the reason he brought it was because it contained a picture of Dr. Green as a young man."

Persimmon Hill, vol. 5, no. 2, 1975. "I remember Doc Green," by Don Hedgpeth. Obituary, and reminiscences of their four-year acquaintanceship. Hedgpeth was the first editor of *Persimmon Hill,* published by The National Cowboy Hall of Fame, located on Persimmon Hill in Oklahoma City, Oklahoma. Hedgpeth says, in part:

"Doc's books were yarns, and they were rooted in the fierce individualism and pride that were for so long the hallmarks of the range country. He wrote just as he talked. It was a key to Doc Green's success. His narratives were full of the juices and vitality of real life. They were not the general run of western writing of recent years that is choked to death by scholarship and bogged stirrup deep in footnotes and bibliography.

"My family visited him at his home in Cumby, Texas. It proved that he was what he seemed. Too many times literary figures and other celebrities affect a public posture to draw attention to themselves. But Doc was the same man at home that he was at any big gathering, where he was often the center of attention.

"His house was a lean-to assembled from various lengths of salvaged lumber and his bed was an old iron cot. He still rolled his bed and his one blue suit hung from an exposed rafter. He was a pretty poor farmer except for his prize peach orchard. Weeds and falling-down fences surrounded the property that his grandfather had homesteaded. He had a large assortment of rabbit hutches and pigeon cages. I will always remember how he took my four-year-old son down to pet the rabbits and scratch a big draft horse's ears.

"One of the things that always bothered Doc was that the popularity he achieved was for what he felt were the wrong reasons. He always thought of himself as an animal scientist, but most folks didn't want to hear about his principles of horse color and conformation, or his ideas about breeding model beef cattle. His fans wanted to hear his horse-swappin' stories and his adventures as a wild, young cowboy in the days when a man could still make a living 'a-horseback.' It is for these stories that he will be remembered.

"One of the major factors in his success as a writer was his personality. I doubt that his books will continue to attract the attention they did when he was around to promote them. But among genuine westerners and their sons and grandsons, there will always be an audience who will read and appreciate the man who wrote stories they could understand, who was indeed one of them.

"Once when he was coming to Oklahoma City, I invited him to stay at our house. He wrote back to say:

" 'I am not too housebroke and make an awful poor guest. . . . I go to bed just after dark and wake up before daylight and wonder if everybody else in the house is dead. By the time I lay there afraid to go to the bathroom — afraid I'll wake somebody up, I have a bad time — so if I make it to the show, you can feed me and I'll camp out somewhere else.'

"That was the Ben K. Green I knew and will remember."

The Dallas Morning News, Saturday, May 1, 1976. Frank X. Tolbert, in "Tolbert's Texas" column headed "Why Hunting Horse Loved the Tongue River Country." Excerpt:

"Other day I was on what is called a 'panel' at the annual meeting of the Texas Folklore Society at the University of Texas at Arlington library. The life and literary works of the late Dr. Ben K. Green were under discussion.

"Ben K. Green was a good friend of mine. I miss the talented old rascal. And also I miss visits to the calm of his Animal Farm, ancestral acres just north of Cumby. The Thoroughbred and Percheron horses and Devon cattle and the sheep and the other animals sometimes seemed almost humanoid in their behavior patterns. Perhaps it was Ben K.'s influence for he loved all the creatures on his farm.

"Once I made some pictures of lambs playing under the feet of huge Percherons. And in one of the pictures it looked as if a mother sheep were talking to one of the horses and telling him not to step on the babies."

Texas Family Land Heritage Registry, First Edition. Texas Department of Agriculture, John C. White, Commissioner, Austin, Texas. 1974. 152 pp, burnt orange stiff paper covers, 8½ by 11 pages.

This handsomely printed book gives a county-by-county description of old family ranches and farms established in Texas prior to 1874. Included in Hopkins County is a description of Ben K. Green's ancestral land, the Pioneer Stock Farm, tracing its ownership from his maternal ancestor, D. W. Cole, who acquired the property in 1849, to Ben K. Green and his uncle, Ben F. Green. The account concludes: "Following the deaths of both Greens in 1974, Miss Juanita Green, sister [aunt?] to Ben K. and niece to Ben F., took control of the 323-acre property."

Acknowledgments

I AM GREATLY INDEBTED to Mrs. Rosemary J. Barker, of Amarillo, Texas, Green's last secretary, who obligingly furnished me with many reproductions of articles, reviews and obituaries; to Mrs. Naomi Scott, of Fort Worth, Ben's first secretary, for information on his stories in the *Quarter Racing Record;* to Miss Margaret Hartley, Editor of the *Southwest Review,* Dallas, for setting the record straight concerning the publication of Ben's first story to appear in the national media; to James K. Howard, former editor of Northland Press, Flagstaff, Arizona, for an extensive listing of reviews from the nation's press; to my friend Willis J. Lutz of Dallas, excellent printer and bibliographer, who called my attention to several obscure appearances of Green's writings; to Mr. Art Hendrix, the able Acquisitions Librarian of East Texas State University, at Commerce, Texas, and to Professor James W. Byrd, Department of Literature and Languages at that fine institution; their appreciation of Ben Green parallels my own; to James C. Martin, Director of Special Collections at The University of Texas at Arlington, Texas, who, with Mrs. Mary Van Zandt of the staff of the Jenkins Garrett Library, have made available to me the extensive collection of Green materials donated to that handsome library by Ben himself shortly before his death.

It is also a pleasure to acknowledge the help and encouragement received from John S. Mayfield, author and lately Librarian at Syracuse University, New York, and now migrating annually between Bethesda, Maryland, and Tyler,

Texas, who has indefatigably tracked down the documentation concerning some little-known episodes in Green's life with a view to an eventual biography; my thanks also to Lee C. Milazzo Jr., Archivist of Southern Methodist University and ardent Dallas bibliophile, who made his rare copy of the uncorrected advance proofs of Green's *Some More Horse Tradin'* available for my examination; and certainly to Frank X. Tolbert, the peripatetic columnist of the *Dallas Morning News,* whose "Tolbert's Texas" column has for many years introduced Doc Green and his "animal farm" to literally thousands of readers.

What a boon it is to have had the help and friendship of such people!

Index

Ben K. Green: A Bibliography
was designed by Robert Jacobson and Paul Weaver,
set in Linotype Granjon with Columbus display,
printed on Mountie Warm White Text
and bound by Roswell Bookbinding, Phoenix